To Grace

Regards
Oscar Nordstrom

Fountain of Change

Fountain of Change

HOW THE LIFE AND IDEAS OF JESUS RESHAPED OUR WORLD

Second Edition

Oscar R. Nordstrom

NorthStream
PUBLISHING

Fountain of Change: How the Life and Ideas of Jesus
Reshaped Our World (Second Edition)

Publication date: May, 2018
Hardcover Edition
ISBN: 978-0-9983109-4-7

Library of Congress Control Number: 2017901503

Manufactured in the United States of America

10 9 8 7 6 5 4 3

Design consultants: South Mountain Studio, LLC
southmountainstudio.com

Interior and Jacket Design by John Clifton, Foley Square Books
foleysquarebooks.com

Cross image on jacket courtesy of The Quiet Witness
thequietwitness.com

North Stream Publishing
52 Old Lake Rd. • Congers, NY 10920.

EMAIL: *info@northstreampublishing.com*
www.northstreampublishing.com

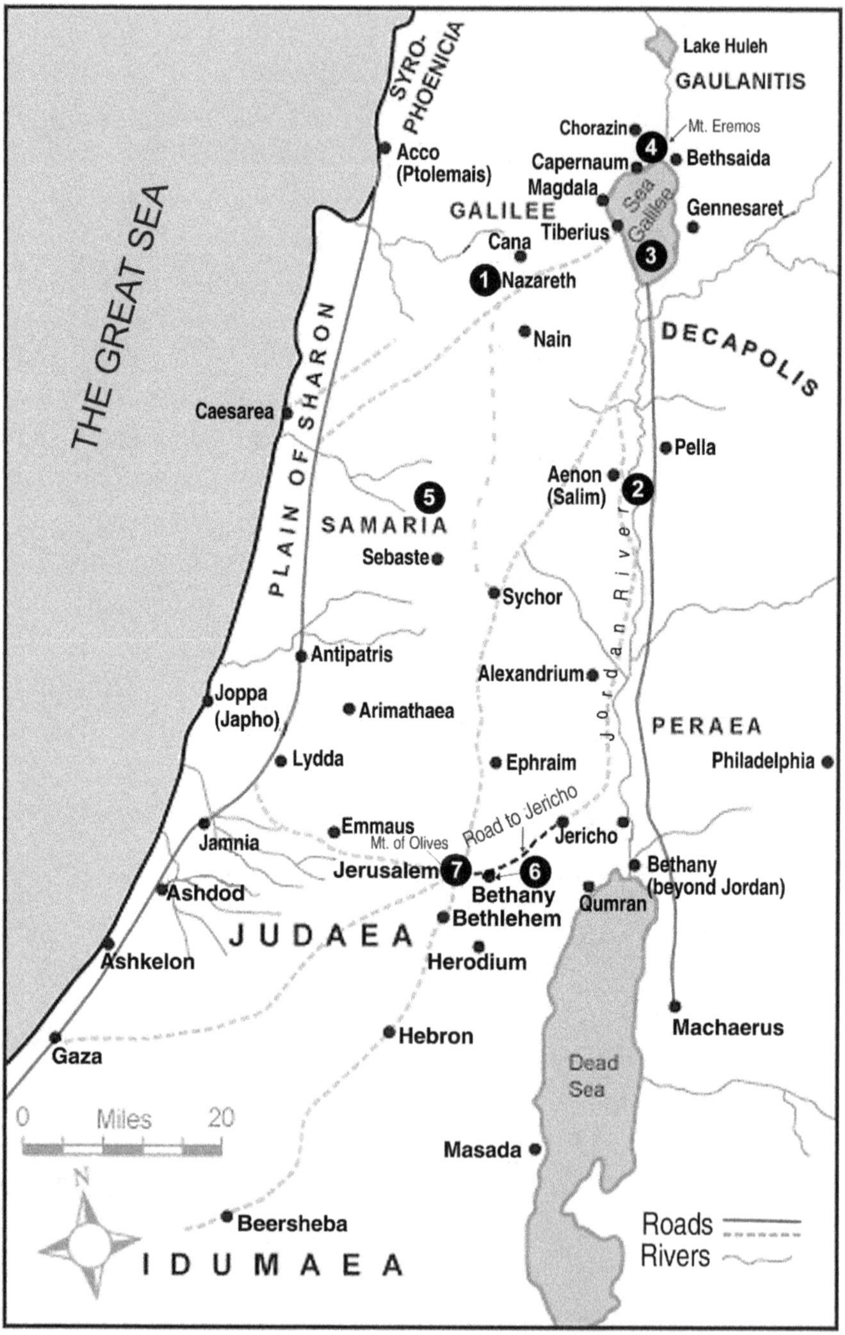

The Holy Land in the Time of Jesus

MAP KEY

1. Nazareth – The Gospels describe Nazareth as the town where Mary and Joseph raised Jesus. (Section* 7, Mt. 13:54-58) The population at the time of Jesus is estimated to have been about 400. *(Israel Antiquities Authority)*

2. Jordan River –156 miles long, flowing south through the Sea of Galilee and Dead Sea. The Gospels tell us that Jesus was baptized in the Jordan by John the Baptist, which marked the start of his public ministry. (Section 7, Mt. 11:2-19 and 14:3-13)

3. Sea of Galilee – The "sea" is a lake about 13 miles long and eight wide. It figures prominently in the Gospels as the place where Jesus chose his first Apostles, and the site of significant events in his life. (Section 3, Mt. 4:18-22)

4. Mount Eremos – Historians point to this location as the site of the "Sermon on the Mount". (Sections 4 through 6)

5. Samaria – Region in Judea and home to the Samaritans, who played an important role in the Gospels. (Section 1, Jn. 4:1-42; Section 11, Lk. 10:29-37)

6. Bethany – Town near Jerusalem mentioned prominently in the Gospels as the home of Mary and Martha, and Jesus' friend Lazarus, whom the Gospels tell us Jesus raised from the dead. (Section 13, Mk. 14:3-7)

7. Jerusalem and Environs – One of the oldest cities in the world and religious and administrative center of Judea dating from the 8th Century B.C. and site of major Gospel passages. (Sections 13-19)

> **Great Temple of Jerusalem** – The Temple and the surrounding plaza (said to have occupied 36 acres at the northeast section of Jerusalem) accommodated huge crowds that came on pilgrimages during Passover. (Section 13)
>
> **The Mount of Olives (Mt. Olivet)** – Named for the olive groves that once covered its slopes, it is within walking distance of the east wall of the Great Temple. The Gospels include several significant events in the life of Jesus that took place there. (Section 14)

8. Road to Jericho – Scene of the "Good Samaritan" (Section 11, Lk. 10:29-37) In the time of Jesus, the road was notorious for its danger and was known as the "Way of Blood." (Wilkinson, *The Way from Jerusalem to Jericho - The Biblical Archaeologist*, Vol. 38, No. 1 (Mar., 1975), pp. 10–24)

•To avoid confusion with the Gospels' use of "Chapter" numbers, this book employs the term "Section" to denote the 21 major parts into which it is divided. (See "CONTENTS" – "Narrative Style and Structure")

Preface

The young man who entered the city gate that day knew he was the target of rich and powerful men who were intent on his destruction. Disregarding the danger that awaited, he walked directly to the place where his words and actions had only recently caused a major disturbance. Though it was early, the sun was already glaring down from a cloudless sky, portending another scorching day in a parched land, with the smells and sounds of animals, the marketplace, and unwashed travelers creating a living mosaic along the way.

The man had come to talk about his beliefs about man's relationship with his Creator and his fellow man, in the certainty that a large audience would be within earshot of his now well-known talent for speaking. He would later become world famous for this gift of oratory, much like other great teachers throughout history, whose philosophies continue to inspire generations long after their voices had fallen silent. Like those of Socrates and other renowned philosophers, this man's teachings were seen as radical. They would be, as he predicted, rejected by many and the source of ridicule and scorn – making him perhaps the most misunderstood man in history, even among many of his own adherents.

While his teachings remain controversial to many, his unique message continues to inspire good throughout the world, even influencing many who do not see him as a great spiritual figure. These would include more than a few of America's founding fathers, who were deists, and more recently, Mahatma Gandhi, a committed Hindu, who once said of him, "To me, [he] was one of the greatest teachers humanity has ever had."[1]

As the young man was speaking that day, an angry mob led by men clad in the garments of their class suddenly descended upon him. These men, whose station was apparent by their proud bearing and the robes and tasseled shawls they wore, were the legal and spiritual leaders of the day, known as Pharisees, Scribes, and Sadducees.[2] The crowd that followed them had all of makings of a latter-day lynch mob. In their midst, a terrified woman in torn garments was half-dragged along. She was a harlot, who had plied her trade as did thousands of others throughout the Roman-dominated world and beyond. There was one difference: the woman had been found guilty of adultery – which mandated a sentence of death by stoning,[3] according to laws laid down to these people some thousands of years before.

The religious leaders had brought the woman to this place for a specific reason. The self-proclaimed savior they were about to confront had been preaching a new order, and the church officials were anxious to dispose of this latest in a long line of religious zealots who had seemingly risen like weeds from the earth that had been blessed as the Jewish homeland since Moses had led the Jews out of captivity. Moreover, they had a plan to do just that. It was based on the very actions and words of the man, including apparent violations of the Sabbath and a litany of interpretations of Jewish law that did not sit well with any of the more learned and affluent Jews of that day.

The church officials were particularly distressed with the man's pronouncements regarding marriage and adultery, which were clear violations of their legal and spiritual laws. While interpreting the meaning of the scriptures had long occupied Jewish scholars, they would never brook the same from others.[4]

The man they sought that day was a carpenter[5] from a tiny

neighboring village, whose growing following might be judged by the Roman overseers as the start of another rebellion. This could have serious repercussions for the entire Jewish population, particularly the titular ruling class, whom the Romans entrusted to keep the always rebellious Jews under control and paying taxes.

The man was tall for his day, approaching six feet, with a presence that commanded attention despite his humble attire. His face and hands bespoke someone accustomed to hard labor in the sun; his dress was a simple coarse homespun linen tunic cinched about the waste with a length of cord. His feet were clad with roughly cut pieces of animal hide. While working men of his day were cautious and submissive by nature, he exuded an air of peaceful confidence, projecting neither arrogance nor servility.

While the man was keenly aware that these civil and religious leaders were forever looking for a means to eliminate him, he remained calm when the crowd approached, and produced the woman. One of the Pharisees said to him, "Teacher, this woman has been found guilty of adultery – what shall we do with her?"

The Pharisees believed they had the man trapped, as they well knew that death by stoning was required by the law, but expected the man to raise his voice against it, given his many pronouncements of love, forgiveness, and redemption. Had he done so in front of so many witnesses, the Pharisees were prepared to accuse him of the crime of setting himself above the law, with as grave a consequence as awaited the woman. Had he not, he would have committed her to being stoned, which he could not do.

How he turned this dilemma into one from which his antagonists could not themselves escape is in itself an amazing story. Moreover, this homespun preacher had often confounded the best religious minds of the day, using scripture to counter the scripture they sought to employ in accusing him. His followers had seen moments like this many times in his short life, and their sharing of these events and the man's message established a legacy that grew after his death into the world's largest religious following.

The man, of course, was Jesus of Nazareth, and the words that saved both the already condemned women and himself from sure death continue to ring in the conscience of all men, even until today. They follow at Page 50 "Jesus' Message of Forgiveness."

Contents

Foreword

Following the publication of *Fountain of Change* (*First Edition*) in March 2017, I had the good fortune to discuss its theme, and other subjects that interested me, on a podcast internet show I hosted on *talkradionyc.com*. During these broadcasts I had occasion to discuss the similarities between Jesus' teachings and the world's other great faiths and spiritual practices, including Hinduism and Buddhism, and even the philosophies of Aristotle and Zeno. If you are interested in hearing any of these broadcasts you can access them at the show's website by clicking on to my show entitled "Off the Beaten Path".

Upon receiving a number positive response to these discussions, I came to the conclusion that I should add material to the first edition to amplify the amazing synergy between Jesus' teachings and that of the world's other belief systems. Since the purpose of *Fountain* is to portray Jesus as a great teacher, philosopher and social reformer outside the trappings of Christendom, what better way to do it than to show how his life and teachings are in concert with the world's most respected moral and philosophical teachings.

As I stated in the original Foreword, *Fountain* was in the making for most of my adult life – all but the recent years without a conscious effort on my part. The impetus to write this book started with the loss of my dear partner and wife to cancer two months past her fifty-eighth birthday. I added that my "recovery" ran the gamut of painful emotions that, thanks to a loving family and friends, finally resolved into a newer and more invested person who came to the startling realization that life had actually dealt me a blow that cleared my head, allowing me to see all the good things that had visited my life, along with the painful ones. Khalil Gibran's *The Prophet* said it best for me in the chapter in which a townswoman asked the Prophet to speak "On Joy and Sorrow." He answered, "Your joy is your sorrow unmasked. The deeper that sorrow carves into your being the more joy you can contain."[6]

And, as they say, while counting my blessings, it came to me that I had piled up a considerable tab, since nothing in this world is truly free. While replaying my life so that I might identify to whom this great debt was owed, it came to me that I could never properly thank those to whom so much was owed, since my wife, mom and dad, teachers, mentors, and many others would no longer be able to open my thank-you notes. Gratefully, I opined, there was someone at the top of that list who I could still thank, and perhaps put a dent in this mountain of IOU's. I hoped that *Fountain of Change* would be a major installment. As I originally prefaced in the first edition, all practicing Christians are painfully aware of the controversies surrounding their faith and the derision with which it has been greeted by many who do not share their beliefs.

And so it was with Jesus' ministry, which was enmeshed in controversy, ridicule, and rejection. He told his followers to expect the same. Things have not changed much. Yet, through all the negativity I have witnessed toward Christianity, more than a bit deservedly so, there has always remained one shining light for me, untouched by all of man's imperfections – the figure of Jesus, whose life was devoted to bringing love, forgiveness, and peace into the world. Having said this begs the question of why so many people clearly harbor contempt for the "Prince of Peace." The answer seems to me to be that, aside from the less than stellar job done by his followers in living up to his principles,[7] they also failed to show the world a perspective of Jesus that most have never seen; for besides being the center of Christianity, Jesus was a wonderful, gifted teacher, philosopher, social reformer, and human being. It is this side of Jesus this book attempts to depict, with limited reference to the religious trappings that surround him. Interestingly, while his followers referred to Jesus as the *"Son of God,"* (Mark 1:1) he always referred to himself as the *"Son of Man."*[8]

Since this book is only intended to illuminate Jesus' teachings and philosophies, it focuses on the three years of his public ministry, from the calling of his Twelve Apostles[9] to his trial and execution and the final words given to his disciples following what Christians believe was his Resurrection. And, because there exists much misunderstanding concerning the mystical Jesus – such as his "Resurrection," the book includes entries and discussion on several of these events, as they will be of some significance to anyone seeking to understand how so many have come to believe in Jesus' divinity. These passages are also needed to provide context to the origin and meaning of more than a quarter of the 40-plus common expressions that have come down to us from the Gospels. Many of these are entered at Page 46, which follows below. These passages include the "Miracle" of the feeding of thousands with five loaves of bread and two fish (at Page 99, below - Matthew 14:3-13) and a discussion of its relationship to the passages which are known as "The Last Supper" (Page

150, Matthew 26:26-30), which was the subject of Da Vinci's world famous mural, and commemorated by Christians as the central part of their daily religious services.

Readers are invited to take whatever meaning these passages have for them and ignore what they see as a distraction from the book's main theme. Finally, while Jesus' message has been vilified by many, misapplied by his adherents, and misunderstood by others, the strength, simplicity, and beauty of his words, when viewed with detachment, will surprise many – and the wisdom of his words and actions will confirm his place among the pantheon of the world's acknowledged great teachers and philosophers. Jesus may even remind his native people of the great biblical figure Solomon.

In a world beset by hate, violence, hostility, and uncertainty, Jesus' teachings offer us a road map and compass to inner peace, happiness, and love.

Narrative Style and Structure

This book is written in narrative style to complement the Gospel passages which convey Jesus' teachings. This was done to help set the scenes for prominent passages found in the Gospels, whose entries are explained in simple terms. These entries are accompanied with a discussion of how they were given prominence by others, as well as their relevance to today's society, and the misunderstandings that some have evoked. The narrative draws on the four original or Canonical Gospels[10] of Matthew, Mark, Luke, and John, whose beginnings can be traced back to the early decades following Jesus' death.

These four books comprise the central part of the over twenty books that make up what Christians refer to as the "New Testament." Only those passages entered hereunder in *italics* and set off in parentheses were copied verbatim from the Gospels. Some phrases were also highlighted in **bold font** for emphasis.

Further, while much of the narration employed is simply an extension of the written text of the Gospels, some entries are based on my own contemplation of certain events which have led to much debate as to their meaning. For example, the Gospels do not explain what or why Jesus began scratching in the dust and dirt with his finger when questioned by the Church officials about the judgment of an adulterous woman, which event is discussed in the Preface of this book – a curious act that has been the subject of a great deal of theological conjecture. Based on my reading of this and other events recorded in the Gospels, I concluded that Jesus had a specific purpose for his action, which is discussed in connection with "Jesus'

Message of Forgiveness."[11]

Where entries such as the above or comments concerning the teachings of the Roman Catholic Church are made, I must emphasize that I do not consider myself a biblical authority, nor a representative of any Christian church. Such entries represent my personal interpretations, which may not agree with the dogma of any of the various Christian denominations, or with any opinion the reader may have, for that matter. These personal observations and commentary are easily distinguishable from the actual liturgy of the Gospels.

Similarly, references to how Jesus' teachings have influenced mankind, and how they may be applied to the modern condition, are based on my own research and contemplation. While it is hoped that these entries are seen as complementary to the book's main theme, no amount of interpretation can alter the wisdom and beauty of the quoted Gospel passages, which are left to the reader's apprehension.

I also added anecdotes that came to mind as I considered the various Gospel passages, and what they might mean to us today. It is hoped that these additions are not viewed as a distraction, but rather serve to kindle similar truths the reader has taken from their life experience. In possible future editions I will endeavor to address all constructive criticisms received.

In addition to the book's many footnotes are numbered end notes which can be found at the end of the book. In addition to identifying citations, these notes are intended to enhance the readers knowledge and enjoyment of the book's many topics.

While relevant portions of biblical passages are entered in the book, others are entered only as citations, *i.e.* Gn.1 (the book of Genesis, Chapter 1), which is the first book of the Judean and

Christian Bibles. If the reader wishes to access any biblical passage noted in the book (including abbreviated titles) they can do so at the Roman Catholic website *www.usccb.org* (click *"Bible"*) or simply by typing in the bible book, chapter (and verse if known) in their web browser, *i.e. Lk 15:11-32* will yield Luke's passage *"The Prodigal Son."*

Finally, since the Gospels identify chapters by number, this book is divided into 21 main "Sections" along with listed subtitles and their corresponding page numbers. The first three numbered Sections 1-3 are general in nature, with Sections 4 through 9 encompassing Chapters 5 through 20 of Matthew's Gospel. Since Matthew is the longest and most detailed of the four Gospels employed in this writing, most of what is written was taken from it. Sections 10, 11, and 12 herein contain selected passages from the Gospels of Mark, Luke, and John in turn. Sections 13-20 cover the remaining Gospel chapters, and include passages taken from all four Gospels. The last section, 21, discusses the rise of Jesus' ministry following his death, and includes common expressions that have come down to us from the writings of Jesus' early converts.

1 Introduction

Jesus' Message is Universal

The name Jesus[12] has come to signify many things to many people over the past two thousand years. Unfortunately, his message of love, peace, and forgiveness has too often been lost amid the human failings that mark man's journey. Because Jesus' message is universal, it is not necessary to view it through the prism of Christianity; his words are sufficiently compelling to warrant contemplation, unadorned. This narrative may show this if the reader can lay aside any preconceptions held about Christianity and simply consider Jesus' word and actions.

Whether you are an atheist, agnostic, of a different faith or subscribe to no belief system makes little difference; Jesus has something to say to each one of us.* If you doubt this, there is a simple question you may ask yourself: If Jesus never existed, or had nothing extraordinary to tell us, how is that today he is universally acknowledged as "The" most famous person who ever lived? So famous in fact that, to the chagrin of many, his name has come into our vernacular to add emphasis to everyday occurrences, and his birth marks our calendar as the year one.

---

* Mahatma Gandhi once wrote, "Because the life of Jesus has the significance and the transcendency to which I have alluded, I believe that he belongs not solely to Christianity, but to the entire world; to all races and people; it matters little under what flag, name or doctrine they may work, profess a faith, or worship a God inherited from their ancestors." —*Modern Review*, October 1941.

Are Jesus' Teachings Unique to Christianity?

Following the publication of *Fountain of Change: How the Life and Ideas of Jesus Reshaped Our World* in March 2017, nationally respected book review organizations confirmed that my goal of portraying Jesus outside of the trappings of Christianity was achieved; *Foreword Reviews*, writing "Nordstrom views the subject in a secular manner; *Midwest Book Review* writing ". . . will be of immense interest to non-Christian readers . . ." and *Kirkus Reviews* writing "The author's aim is to treat Jesus as a moral philosopher and a social reformer, just as one might study the teachings of Buddha or the Rev. Martin Luther King Jr."

Kirkus' review put me in mind to examine what the other great faiths and philosophies of the world might have in common with Jesus' teachings in more detail than I had when researching *Fountain*, which contains numerous references on the subject. Since Islam, Buddhism, Hinduism and Judaism all originated in the East, or Asia Minor, it was not altogether surprising to find striking similarities between Jesus teachings and these other great faiths which, with Christianity, encompass more than 90% of the world's religious followers. What proved more surprising was finding what Jesus' teachings have in common with some of the world's great philosophers including Aristotle and Zeno. Also, one of Christianity's greatest and universally respected theologians, Saint Thomas Aquinas, studied Virgil and Cicero. Perhaps the most surprising was to find that the idea of this universality had so fascinated the great American mythologist Joseph Campbell that his *magnum opus* "Hero with a Thousand Faces" explored the subject of comparative mythology and religion, wherein Jesus is likened to many religious and mystical heroes whose stories contained a similar pattern.

Jesus' Connection to Mythology - Joseph Campbell's "Hero with a Thousand Faces"

Campbell's book tells of the epic tales of heroes who helped mankind overcome human weaknesses and suffering. He wrote that mankind's saviors included Osiris, who was Egyptian's God of death and eternal life; Krishna, the Hindu Supreme Being and teacher; Prometheus, the Greek God who defied Zeus to feed and protect mankind; Buddha, who taught how man could overcome suffering; Moses, who was the lawgiver and freed God's chosen from bondage; Mohammad, who proselytized belief in the one true God, Allah; and Jesus, who was the destroyer of death. (See pages 122 and 143)

Interestingly, Campbell's writings greatly influenced George Lucas' *Star Wars*, C.S. Lewis *Travels of Narnia*, JRR Tolkien *Lord of the Rings* and J. K. Rowling's *Harry Potter* Books. Not coincidentally, each of these writers have confirmed that they were heavily influenced by the figure and teachings of Jesus as well.

Aristotle and Saint Thomas Aquinas

Thomas Aquinas was an Italian Dominican friar whose influence on Western thought is considerable. Thomas sought to reconcile Aristotle's philosophies with the principles taught by Jesus and is honored as a saint by the Roman Catholic Church, who considers him as its greatest theologian and philosopher, as well as the model teacher for those studying for the priesthood.

Zeno* and the Apostle Paul

During his stay in Athens, the Apostle Paul began debating

---

* Contemporary of Alexander the Great

Epicurean's and followers of Zeno in a public square (*Book of Acts*). In his letters to new Gentile converts, Paul used his knowledge of stoicism* to help these early converts understand the nature of Christianity. Another Christian who wrote of the impact that stoicism had upon Christianity was Bishop Ambrose of Milan – who, although looked on as a great philosopher of the church, is most famous for the line "When in Rome, do as the Roman's do."

Marcus Aurelius and the Anglican Priest Maxwell Staniforth

In the introduction to Marcus Aurelius' *Meditations* Staniforth discusses the influence that stoicism had upon the Roman Emperor and his writings to himself for self-improvement, later made into a book entitled *Meditations*. In the introduction, Staniforth also discusses the profound effect that stoicism had upon Christianity.

St. Augustine Studied Virgil, Cicero and Hinduism

St. Augustine was an important theologian and philosopher whose 4th century writings were of significance to such as philosophers Schopenhauer, Kierkegaard, and Nietzsche, as well as St. Thomas Aquinas. St. Augustine, who also studied both Virgil and Cicero, and once said "We never cease to look toward India, where many things are proposed for our admiration."

---

* The word stoic from Stoicism, as was practiced in the ancient world is far different from our modern definition which defines a stoic as someone who is unmoved by pain and pleasure. Stoicism, as originally practiced, actually espoused that our passions be controlled by reason. And rather than extinguishing emotion, they taught to control it by reason, logic, reflection and concentration so as to develop clear judgement and inner calm.

Hinduism and Jesus' Teachings

So striking are the similarity between Hinduism[13] and the teachings of Jesus that some have claimed that Jesus traveled to India and was there exposed and influenced by its teachings. In fact, Mahatma Gandhi[14] said he could find no difference between the *Sermon on the Mount* and the *Bhagavad Gita*, one of Hinduism's most sacred scriptures. Both call their adherents to follow a moral code dedicated to non-violence, forgiveness, love of one's neighbor, charity, detachment from the self and from the world, and self-control. The similarities of the teachings may explain why Hindu's not only respect and honor Jesus and his mother Mary as deities, but most can recite the "*Lord's Prayer*" (the "*Our Father*").

Buddhism and Jesus' Teachings

On the surface there appears to be little similarity between Buddhism and the teachings of Jesus.[15] However, if we look deeper we will find that there are striking similarities. This was brought home most cogently by two of Buddhism's modern leading figures. In fact, the Dalai Lama, arguably the world's most famous Buddhist, has had a great deal of dialogue with Christians on interfaith issues, including in six meetings with Pope John Paul II. In 1996 the Dalai Lama published *The Good Heart: A Buddhist Perspective on the Teachings of Jesus,* wherein he drew parallels between Jesus and Buddha. The book followed a conference, two years earlier, with members of the Anglican Church of England wherein he remarked that he saw many parallels between Buddhism and the teachings of Jesus, at one-point saying: "one could almost say that these passages could be introduced into a Buddhist text, and they would not even be recognized as traditional

Christian scriptures."[16]

Another famous Buddhist, Thich Nhet Hahn, a Buddhist Monk and internationally known author and lecturer spent years living with Christians and sharing the common threads of Buddhism and the teachings of Jesus. In 1999 Hahn wrote the well-regarded book *Going Home – Jesus and Buddha as Brothers*. Commenting on the book, the Washington Post wrote that the books message was that peace, love, and compassion are central to the teachings both faiths.

One result of these dialogues is that numerous Catholic priests, monks and nuns have visited Dharamshala, India, to learn methods of concentration and meditation from Buddhism, and several Buddhist monks have taught in Catholic Seminaries. Significantly, many Christians and Jews now see no conflict in practicing Buddhist meditation, as well as its principles of morality and awareness of one's responsibilities to supplement their religious practice. Some churches are now teaching meditation.

Islam, Judaism and Jesus' Teachings

It is important to note at the start that the followers of all three faiths believe in the same God, whether we call him Allah, God or Yahweh, and the three faiths see Abraham as the father from which their groups sprang. In addition, all three faiths believe in the prophets of the Old Testament, divine revelation, heaven, angels, Satan and hell. All are also charged to follow a code of moral responsibility and accountability, which will be weighed on Judgment Day, leading to eternal reward or punishment.

Judaism and Jesus

While Christians believe that Jesus came to save the Jews, as well as all of mankind, virtually all Jews have only seen persecution at the hands of Jesus' followers. And while Jesus considered himself to be learned and devout Jew and was referred to as "Rabbi" (teacher) by both his followers and, according to the Gospels, the Church hierarchy who opposed him, as they believed his claim to be the son of God was heresy. As stated in *Fountain's* first edition, while Jesus held the Church officials in contempt for what he saw as an abuse of their power and a failure to faithfully follow God's laws,[17] they clearly believed that Jesus was a false prophet and not the Messiah whose coming was foretold in the Old Testament. Finally, while Jews have been persecuted throughout history for their beliefs,* it must be remembered that Christianity itself started out as a Jewish religious order, and virtually all of Jesus' disciples and early followers were themselves Jews.

Islam and Jesus

The Islamic faith was spread by the armies of Mohammad[18] who Muslims (the name means those who submit to the will of Allah) revere Jesus as the last great prophet and messenger of God before Muhammad. Muslims also believe that Jesus was the Messiah (or the Christ), sent to guide the Children of Israel with a new revelation. Like many Christians, Muslims believe that Jesus was conceived by the virgin Mary, who is revered in her own

---

* I addressed the wrongful persecution of Jews, who many Christians wrongfully blamed for the death of Jesus, in the first edition of *Fountain of Change* (See page 157)

right, and that he didn't marry or have any children. Interestingly, the name Jesus appears more often than Mohammad in the Quran, where he is given various titles, including as the "Son of Mary"

In Islamic theology, Jesus is believed to have performed many miracles, several being mentioned in the Quran. Like all prophets in Islamic tradition, Jesus is also called a Muslim, as he preached that his followers should follow the "straight path." Jesus is written about by some Muslim scholars as the "perfect man," something Mahatma Gandhi also believed. However, Muslims do not believe that Jesus was crucified, but was instead was raised alive from the temple mount in Jerusalem to heaven.

Historicity of Jesus

Scholars of ancient history (both Christian and non-Christian)[19] who have studied the historical records that survived from the early centuries following Jesus' death have concluded that there is no question that the Jesus described in the Gospels existed. Moreover, virtually all scholars of antiquity agree that there are multiple sources that confirm Jesus was a Jew born in Galilee, was baptized by John the Baptist, and was crucified at the command of Pontius Pilate, the Roman Prefect of Judea, because of confrontations with the Jewish leaders of that time. Most scholars of antiquity also agree that Jesus was born between 6 and 3 BC (Before Christ), and was crucified between AD 30 and 33 (from the Latin *anno Domino* - literally "The Year of Our Lord") and that his followers spread his message throughout much of the Roman Empire after he died.

The difficulty in dating Jesus' exact date of birth is partially due to differences between the accounts included in the Gospels

– which is understandable, since the Gospels were written sometime after Jesus' death, and there is no actual record of his birth and little record of his early life. Another factor is that the first attempt to calculate his birth was apparently not recorded by the church until the year 525. Moreover, the convention of dating history as the terms "AD" and "BC"[20] did not take hold until after the year AD 800. However, since this writing will focus on Jesus' teachings, no further discussion on the subject is required.

Finally, while there have been many questions raised concerning the lack of non-Christian historical records concerning Jesus' life and teachings, it should be remembered that the Jewish and Roman leaders of Jesus' time would have considered him just another minor rebel who died an ignominious death following three short years of public ministry in a remote area of the vast Roman Empire. It is therefore not surprising that few historical records from that period took note of Jesus' life and passing until his followers began to be slaughtered *en masse*.

Historicity of the Gospels

There is also some disagreement as to the exact dates when the Gospels were written. However, historians agree that there is considerable circumstantial evidence that the first Gospel (Mark) was written less than thirty years after Jesus' death, based upon fragments that have been found. Moreover, the foretelling of the razing of the Great Temple in Jerusalem described in Mark as occurring at some future date, (which did occur in AD 70) clearly indicates it was written before the event otherwise, Mark would ostensibly have used the actual year of the event to support Jesus' prediction of its destruction.

That Jesus' life and ministry were not committed to writing sooner is not surprising, since the original Apostles were not men of letters; in fact it appears that none of the Gospels were written by the Apostles themselves, but rather by early converts who accompanied them during their ministry. These details are entered in the introductions to each of the four canonical [21] Gospels of Matthew (Mt.), Mark (Mk.), Luke (Lk.), and John (Jn.) that follow. The first three Gospels are also known as the Synoptic Gospels because of their similarity. The fourth, John, appears to have been written as an instructional for the faithful, whereas the first three are more of a record of Jesus' life and follow the events that occurred in chronological order.

It is also well established that oral tradition in earlier times preceded the written among the poorer classes, since many could not read or write, and papyrus was not readily available to the working class. This is undoubtedly why the earliest records we have of Jesus' life are contained in letters written by early converts to Christianity, such as Saul of Tarsus, later Saint Paul – whose Epistles (letters) date to within twenty-five years of Jesus' death. Readers may be familiar with one of Paul's letters to the inhabitants of Corinth, an isle off the coast of Greece, whose opening line reads: "If I speak in human and angelic tongues but do not have love, I am a resounding gong or a clashing cymbal" (1 Cor. 13).*

A significant issue that confronts many regarding Jesus' teachings is that skeptics have long held that some, if not all, of

---

* The King James Version may be more familiar to the reader; the opening line reads: "Though I speak with the tongues of men and of angels, and have not charity, I am become as sounding brass, or a tinkling cymbal."

the Gospels were fabricated, in part because certain accounts of events depicted differ from one Gospel to another, and the words Jesus uses in his teachings also vary among the four Gospels. However, authorities on the subject believe these differences do not detract from their authenticity but rather *support* it, for good reason. Firstly, the Gospels were provably written at different times by different people. Moreover, the Gospels clearly demonstrate that Jesus preached the same doctrine on more than one occasion to different groups, making it likely that several evangelists recounted what they had heard or been told with some degree of variation. If the Gospels had been fabricated, the presumption is that they would be in closer agreement with each other.

Of further significance, many historians agree that the Gospels comply with accepted theories employed to confirm the authenticity of ancient documents, such as the "Criterion of Multiple Attestation" (independent supporting sources); the "Criterion of Coherence" (writing agrees with known facts); the "Criterion of Embarrassment,"[22] and other supporting facts, including that the Gospels employed Aramaic language and structure in use at that time. Further, the Gospels reflect the socioeconomic and political/religious practices at that time. Interestingly, while the *Dead Sea Scrolls*, which were written in the second century by a small sect of monastic Jews known as the Essenes, do not mention Jesus, their form and phraseology matches that of the Gospels.

Based in no small part on the above, there is near unanimous agreement amongst theologians and scholars of antiquity that it is extremely unlikely that the Gospels were after-the-fact fabrications of a few individuals.

Further, those who doubt that the Gospels accurately reflect Jesus' words and actions might consider the fact that Socrates left no written record of his life and teachings. While he is acknowledged as one of the founders of Western Philosophy, his teachings are only available to us through the writings of his disciples, Plato and Xenophon, and contemporaries Aristotle and Aristophanes. Similarly, Jesus' teachings are only available to us through the Gospels and letters written by educated early converts, such as Saul of Tarsus (St. Paul) and Licinius (St. Luke), a Syrian/Greek Physician.

Finally, while the reader may wish to question the authenticity of the Gospels, the beauty and wisdom they convey remains as valid as any work conveyed to us from antiquity. Nor does the strength of Jesus' message require belief in his divinity. However, as entered in the book's Foreword it was necessary to include a brief description of a few of the miracles that have been attributed to Jesus to give context to significant passages which may be of interest to the reader.

Jesus' Rise from Obscurity Following His Crucifixion

How Jesus came to prominence, given the obscurity of his brief life and ignominious death, is an amazing story, particularly considering the following facts.*

- Jesus was born in a tiny village in Judea, a remote area of the world then governed by the Roman Empire.
- From what we know of his brief life (he died between the age of 33 and 36), his

* Facts taken from various publications and websites – see "CREDITS" starting at page 178.

public ministry lasted only a few years and gathered little attention, much of which was unfavorable, as he was branded a rabble-rouser and heretic by the Jewish leaders of his day.

- Jesus never traveled far from where he was born, nor was he a man of property or wealth.
- Jesus never held an office or was acknowledged by anyone of station.
- Jesus left no direct written record to posterity.
- After his brief ministry, Jesus was tried by the Roman Prefect of Judea, Pontius Pilate, and condemned to death.
- Jesus was crucified, a sentence given the worst criminals of that time.

Considering the obscurity and controversy of his brief ministry, the fact that Jesus rose to prominence *after* he died is remarkable. Jews have thousands of years of tradition from their father Abraham - to their law-giver Moses - to Malachi, the forty-seventh book of what Christians refer to as the "Old Testament."[23] Islam was spread by the sword of its great Prophet Muhammad. Buddha's philosophies became famous during the 45 years he traveled throughout Eastern India. Other faiths have similarly long formative histories.

Following his death, there was no one of prominence to carry forth his message, only members of his original Apostles, and some of those whose lives he came to touch. And from what the Gospels tell us about his immediate followers, some were women, who were forbidden from speaking in public, one Apostle committed suicide (Matthew 27:3-10 – Page 154), another was a despised and shunned tax collector, and the others were poor, uneducated fishermen and lower class tradesmen who understandably scattered in fear following his arrest and crucifixion.

Surely none of his immediate followers had the authority to inspire the movement that has led to the largest single religious following in the world today.[24] All they had was the power and beauty of Jesus' teachings and their belief in a preternatural event that inspired these few simple men to give up their lives, so that Jesus words might live.[25]

Jesus' Influence on Humanity

That Jesus is the most influential figure in world history is incontestable. Not only does he continue as the most universally recognizable figure in the world, but his teachings have resulted in the greatest *cultural* revolution of all time. In fact, if he were never seen as a great spiritual founder of Christianity, he would unquestionably be hailed today as one of the greatest moral and ethical teachers, social reformers, philosophers, and humanitarians in the history of the world, including by many who do not subscribe to the religious beliefs of his followers.

John F. Kennedy, the widely admired 35th President of the United States, in his 1961 inaugural address famously said ". . . ask not what your country can do for you, ask what you can do for your country." Jesus could have easily said the same thing, only he would have used the word "mankind" in lieu of "your country." Surely no one can doubt that many of his followers were, and continue to be, inspired to enlist in Jesus' *Peace Corps.*

No one should doubt that Jesus' teachings have profoundly influenced the course of human history and affected the lives of billions of Christians and non-Christians alike, including

Muslims – who consider Jesus a great prophet. Certainly, a listing of history's most famous and influential people would be meaningless if it were to exclude individuals who identified themselves as Christians.

Moreover, Jesus' teachings have given rise to the most-read book in history, and his personage has been the inspiration for many universally admired Christian figures, including Saint Francis of Assisi, Saint Augustine[26] (whose seminal work *Grace and Free Will* answers the age-old theological question of predestination. Saint Augustine's inspired answer: "If God has not given us free will why then did he give us the Ten Commandments?"), and Saint Thomas Aquinas, who sought to combine the philosophy of Aristotle with the theology of the Church. More recently, much of the world has honored Pope John Paul II, Mother Teresa of Calcutta, and Pope Francis I.

In addition, more world-famous works of architecture, art, and music have been created to honor Jesus than anyone in world history. That influence was captured in the soaring, stained glass cathedrals in Europe, as well as the world-famous paintings and sculptures of the Renaissance, including Michelangelo's *La Pieta* and his painting of the Sistine Chapel and Da Vinci's *Last Supper*.

Many of the world's greatest authors' and composers' works were inspired by Jesus, such as G. F. Handel's *Messiah*, one of the best known and most frequently performed choral works in our time; Franz Schubert's *Ave Maria*; and John Newton's *Amazing Grace*, which was inspired by Thomas à Kempis's *The Imitation of Christ*. Another Renaissance figure inspired by Jesus was Dante Alighieri, whose *Divine Comedy* is viewed as one of the greatest works in world literature.

Other famous composers and authors who self-identified themselves as devout Christians include Wolfgang Amadeus Mozart, Johan Sebastian Bach, Leo Tolstoy, Fyodor Dostoevsky, Søren Kierkegaard, John Milton, Charles Dickens and in more modern times, John Updike, Vaclav Havel, J.R.R. Tolkien (*Lord of the Rings*), C. S. Lewis (*The Chronicles of Narnia*), and perhaps even J. K. Rowling (the *Harry Potter* series. See Page 122).

In addition, many of the world's greatest scientists publicly identified themselves as Christians and a number stated that their beliefs were relevant to the development of their work. The most famous of this group include Nicolaus Copernicus, Galileo Galilei,[27] Johannes Kepler, Sir Isaac Newton, René Descartes, Robert William Boyle, Francis Bacon (a Franciscan Friar), André-Marie Ampère, Alessandro Volta, Michael Faraday, and Louis Pasteur. Moreover, the listing of church clergy who have made major contributions to the sciences and medicine numbers into the hundreds. This is not surprising since the Roman Catholic Church, by far the largest Christian group, does not disparage reason, but rather encourages it. It is therefore not surprising that that a scientific breakthrough like the "Big Bang" theory,* now prevalent among cosmologists, was first proposed by Georges Lemaître, a Belgian Priest – or that Gregor Mendel, an Augustinian Friar, developed theories in genetics (before the field was given its name) and contributed to the development of the theory of evolution, which is accepted by the Roman Catholic Church and taught in its parochial schools.

Jesus' influence on America was also profound, with many of

---

* Interestingly, the Jewish philosopher Nahmanides wrote that the universe expanded from the time of its creation, at which point it was the size of a mustard seed.

America's founding fathers and virtually all our Presidents espousing Christian ideals. Many other world leaders have expressed similar ideals, including Mahatma Gandhi, who was a great admirer of Jesus.[28] Gandhi's non-violence, non-cooperation movement influenced Martin Luther King Jr. Interestingly, Dr. King once said of Gandhi, "It is ironic, yet inescapably true, that the greatest Christian of the modern world was a man who never embraced Christianity."[29]

This list could go on, but if you are not now persuaded that Jesus has something of significance to tell us, then you would not be persuaded by ten thousand more examples.

Jesus' Teachings Are Relevant Today

Although the reader may believe Jesus' teachings are out of touch in our modern world, those who read this narrative may find them as timely today as they were when he walked the hills of Galilee, almost two thousand years ago. This should not surprise anyone who still finds wisdom in the works of many figures from antiquity, such as Cicero, Marcus Aurelius, and the great Greek philosophers who preceded Jesus, such as Socrates, Plato, Zeno, and Aristotle, whose teachings were embraced by the great Christian theologian, Saint Thomas Aquinas.*

While the purpose of this writing is simply to convey the words Jesus spoke during his public ministry as they have come down to

---

* Saint Thomas Aquinas was as an Italian Dominican friar whose influence on Western thought is considerable. Thomas embraced several ideas put forward by Aristotle, whom he referred to as "the Philosopher," and sought to reconcile Aristotle's philosophies with the principles of Christianity. Thomas is honored as a saint by the Roman Catholic Church and is considered its greatest theologian and philosopher, as well as the model teacher for those studying for the priesthood.

us in the Gospels, it is altogether fitting to include references to those who have been influenced by those words, and to discuss both their relevance in today's society and the controversies which some have occasioned as well.

Jesus as a Secular Man and Social Reformer

Most people see Jesus as purely a religious figure; however, while the purpose of the Gospels was to convey Jesus as the savior of mankind, they also portray a man who was poetic (Mt. 5:1-12), forgiving (Jn. 8:7), and while meek and humble (Mt. 11:29), a fearless fighter for justice (Lk. 10:29). The Gospels also tell us of a Jesus who could be sarcastic (Mt. 16:1-12), angry (Mk.3:5), and filled with doubt (Mt. 26:26-36); someone who could weep (Jn. 11:35) and even be moved to violence (Mt. 21:12-17).

Moreover, Jesus was a social reformer who was almost two millennia ahead of his time in his respect for women (See Page 41); in preaching that we should love our neighbor (Mt. 22:39); in the concept of a trial by one's peers (Mt. 8:15), and in regard to fostering and protection of children (Mt. 18:1-5, 6-9; 19:13-15).

Do Christians Accept the Gospels as "Gospel?"

While all Christians accept the Gospels as inviolable, some contend that they must be understood exactly as written, without any possibility of interpretation. However, there are several contending facts that provide a reasonable basis for believing otherwise, not the least of which is that there are discernible differences among the Gospels regarding events in the life of Jesus, including the circumstances of his birth, and other significant events. While this would seem to call into question the authenticity of the Gospels, the opposite is true, as noted at Page 26 above, "Historicity of the Gospels."

Another fact to be considered is that the Gospels were written and translated from ancient Hebrew, Aramaic, Latin, and Greek writings at different times, by different individuals, resulting in variations among the Gospels themselves and among the various Christian Bibles such as the King James Version (KJV) and Roman Catholic Bible.[30] In addition, various Christian denominations deem certain religious writings as apocryphal, while others give those writings status as part of the New Testament.

Further, the language spoken at the time of Jesus did not contain the precision of today's English, so translators had to interpret certain words, which had a profound effect upon their import and fundamental beliefs among various Christian groups throughout history, continuing even until today. Two significant examples are discussed in the section "Did Jesus Condemn Non-Christians?" which follows directly. Another example can be found in the Greek word *cheir*, found in the original Gospels. *Cheir* could mean hand, wrist, or forearm. This may explain why virtually all earlier depictions of Jesus' crucifixion *incorrectly* showed nails driven through the palm of his hands, whereas we now know that the Romans drove nails through the wrists.

Also, neither the Hebrew nor the Greek language had a separate word for "sibling" and "cousin." This may be the basis for the belief that Jesus had brothers and sisters[31] (Matthew 13:54-58, Page 97).

Moreover, language is dynamic; terms, phraseology and sentence structure once common to our immediate ancestors have fallen away. A convincing example can be found in the works of Shakespeare, which although written some 1,500 years after Jesus' death, require numerous footnotes for those who want to fully understand the dialogue.

Of greater significance, Jesus frequently used parables* (from the Greek *parabolé*, meaning comparison, illustration, analogy) to teach his followers. Interestingly, the Greek word *parabolé* was translated from the Hebrew word *mashal*, which can also mean "riddle." This seems to bear more than passing consideration, as Jesus told his disciples that they only were given the ability to understand the full meaning of the parables.[32] And so, while Jesus used common subjects in his parables and proverbial expressions, the underlying messages were profound, witness the oft repeated reference to the mustard seed.[33]

Of no less importance, if the Gospels are not to be subject to interpretation, then are the works of the great biblical scholars and saints, whose lives were devoted to a better understanding of Jesus' teachings and their application to man's condition, to be without merit? Indeed, Saint Thomas Aquinas wrote: "The ultimate goal of theology is to use reason to grasp the truth about God."

Finally, it is not necessary for the reader to consider whether the words of the Gospel are inviolate, as the purpose of this book is only to amplify Jesus' teachings. And given the nature of the parables, it is hoped that the reader will gain a richer and deeper understanding of Jesus' message through the application of their own life experiences to the contemplation of the Gospel passages. There is a great truth regarding this which says that "meaning is not in words, but in people." Surely, the

---

* Parables occupy about one-third of the Gospel's main themes, numbering between thirty-three and sixty, if proverbial expressions such as "the salt of the Earth" are included.

spirit of Jesus' teachings is more important than the words that seek to define them.

Did Jesus Condemn Non-Christians?

Some Christian denominations believe that those who do not accept Jesus' divinity are condemned to damnation. This belief is founded upon certain passages in the Gospels, including:

(a) John 3:3, wherein we must all be "born again" (KJV) in Jesus to have eternal life;

(b) John 14:6, wherein Jesus tells his disciples,

> *"I am the way and the truth and life. No one comes to the Father except through me"*

(c) Mark 16:16, wherein Jesus says to his Apostles,

> *"Whoever believes and is baptized will be saved; whoever does not believe will be condemned."*

While the above passages, and similar ones found in John 3:36 and 7:38 and elsewhere, appear to support this belief, there are Christian denominations, including the largest, the Roman Catholic Church, that do not share this view. Because of the controversial nature of this issue felt by Christian and non-Christians alike, the following is a brief discussion of the cited passages, and a recital of other Gospel passages that are supportive of the view that Jesus did not condemn non-believers.

(a) The term "born again" occurs in John 3:3 (KJV) as part of a passage wherein a Pharisee named Nicodemus tells Jesus he believes that he has come from God, because no one could do the things that he is doing unless it were so. Jesus' response, in part, (as recorded in the Roman Catholic Bible) advises Nicodemus that one must be *"born from above"* to see God's kingdom.

The difference in wording ("born again" vs. *born from above*) derives from the fact that the Greek adverb *anóthen*, from which the translation is taken, can mean both "from above" and "again." The translation *born from above* appears to be reinforced in John 3:31. While the distinction may not seem great, Catholic theologians have concluded the passage was meant for all men, who, moved by the grace of God "from above," may enter heaven. [34]

(b) Jesus' words (John 14:6) were spoken at the time of the "Last Supper" (Page 149). In the cited passage, Jesus tells his Apostles that he is to die soon, but that he is going to prepare a place for them, and that they will "*know the way.*" Upon hearing this, the Apostle Thomas, who would later earn the title "Doubting Thomas" (Page 167, John 20:24-29), says to Jesus:

> *"Master, we do not know where you are going; how can we know the way?" (John 14:5).*

Jesus' reply, as entered above, was clearly intended to respond to Thomas' doubt. Catholic doctrine holds that a fuller meaning of the entire discourse is that Jesus' words here were intended to convey to his Apostles that God, the Father, was manifested in the person and works of Jesus, and that he was therefore the truth and "*the way*" for his Apostles.

Further, if John 14:6 is viewed in the context of Jesus as the final judge through whom "*all*" must pass (St. Peter's Gate?) to be with the Father in heaven (Page 56 - Matthew 25:31-34), his words to his Apostles take on an entirely different meaning.

(c) Jesus used the words entered above (Mark 16:16) in his final address to his Apostles as he commissioned them to go into the world and bring his words to "*all nations*" (Matthew 28:16-20) and "*every creature*" (Mark 16:15). Therefore, these words, when taken in context, can only apply to those to whom these inspired Apostles reached directly. Indeed, the power of this commission is evident in the vast numbers of people who became followers after receiving Jesus' disciples.

In contrast with the above, there are other equally compelling passages that indicate Jesus did not condemn those who did not know him or believe in his divinity. For example, in Matthew 8:5-13 Jesus is approached by a Roman Centurion who asks that he heal a servant in such a humble manner that Jesus is "*amazed*" and says:

> *"I say to you, many will come from the east and the west, and will recline...at the banquet in the kingdom of heaven."*

In John 12:47, Jesus tells a crowd

> *"And if anyone hears my words and does not observe them, I do not condemn him, for I did not come to condemn the world but to save the world."*

In John 10:16 Jesus says *"I have other sheep, that do not belong to this fold."* In Luke 12:42-48, Jesus gives a gathered crowd a parable about a faithful servant (one who observes God's laws), whom he contrasts with an unfaithful and abusive servant who would be severely beaten (cast into hell) when the master returned. But Jesus adds:

> *"And the servant who was ignorant of his master's will but acted in a way deserving of a severe beating shall be beaten only lightly."*

Other New Testament passages also speak of Jesus coming to save all mankind, including those recorded in a letter written by St. Paul:

> *"For this we toil and struggle, because we have set our*

> *hope on the living God, who is the savior of all, especially of those who believe." (1 Timothy 4:10).*

Here St. Paul, arguably the most influential of all of Jesus' disciples, clearly recognizes both believers and nonbelievers as recipients of God's love and mercy.

While Jesus clearly denounced those who committed sins against God or mankind, which he saw as the same, there are no Gospel passages in which he condemned those of other faiths or those who had not yet received his message. Indeed, the latter would encompass much of the world's population from the birth of mankind to the present, a view that on its face seems implausible, given the nature of the personage of Jesus as depicted in the Gospels. Indeed, Jesus preached love, even of one's enemies (Luke 23:34), tolerance, and forgiveness even for the Roman soldiers who crucified him and the crowd that condemned him (Luke 23:34).

Finally, all discerning individuals do not simply accept what others tell them to believe, but rather trust in what their own life experiences and insights instruct. If that instruction does not persuade someone of good conscience, such as Mahatma Gandhi, to believe in the divinity of Jesus, how can one find that sinful or deserving of eternal damnation? Faith, like love, is not a free choice; it comes and goes through forces beyond our control and understanding, and is part of human nature. How could a loving Jesus condemn a man or woman for being human?

How Did Jesus View Women and Children?

The Gospels contain many stories of Jesus' interaction with women, including those of other faiths (Mk. 7:24-30; Jn. 1:1-42) and the prominent role they played in his ministry. Moreover, given the low status held by women in Jesus' time, the very fact that the Gospels repeatedly record his view of women as individuals[35] rather than as members of a lesser class is remarkable. In Luke 13:16, Jesus illuminates his respect for women, referring to them as "daughters of Abraham" in much the same way that Jewish men (and later Christians and Muslims) consider themselves "Sons" of Abraham. This is unique among the western world's faiths.

Jesus' view on the protection and welfare of children is just as pronounced, and like that of women, more than two thousand years ahead of its time. There are many Gospel passages regarding this important topic, several of which will be discussed in some detail later, including in Matthew 18:1-5 (Page 106). Other similarly distinctive passages not recorded hereunder can be found in the Gospels (Mk. 5:21-43, Mk. 7:24-30, Mk. 10:13-16, Lk. 7:36-50, Lk. 8: 1-3, Lk. 10:13-17, Lk. 15: 8-10, and Lk.18:15-17). The love that Jesus had for children and his striking admonitions against harming them sits in sharp contrast to the abuse many have suffered at the hands of clergy members. This will be discussed under Matthew 19:13-15, "Jesus Blesses the Children" on Page 110.

While many passages confirming Jesus' respect for women are contained within the Gospels, a few of which are recorded in the main body of this book,[36] this subject is of such significance to modern society as to warrant discussion as a separate topic. The following passages are entered accordingly. . . .

Jesus and the Woman of Samaria (John 4:1-42)

This passage tells of Jesus meeting a woman at a well in a town in Samaria. Jesus, wearied from his journey, stops at the well to rest where a woman has come to draw water. When Jesus asks her to give him a drink, she is surprised and asks why he would make such a request, as it was known that Jews had no interaction with Samaritans.[37] Jesus' response draws her into a lengthy discussion, which crosses several strict conventions that proscribed a Jew from talking freely to any woman – let alone a scorned Samaritan widow who confesses to living with a man to whom she was not married. Further, asking for a drink from her cup, which had not been ritually cleansed, was also a departure from Jewish law. However, the greatest breach occurred when Jesus discussed theological matters with her, which elicited her shameful admission.

While this story may seem unremarkable when viewed through the mores of today's Western society, the meeting represented a significant breach of social and religious observances of the day. Clearly, Jesus was ahead of his time in his respect and reverence for women. Of no small significance, Jesus' words and actions risked alienating the very people among whom he sought to make followers. Even his Apostles upon their joining Jesus *"marveled"* that he was talking to this woman (John 4:27).

These entries and similarly provocative actions taken by Jesus throughout his short life are one of the reasons he told his followers to expect that his ministry would be ridiculed and rejected by many, and that he had come not to make peace, but rather to challenge the existing norms.[38] In fact, his ideas were so radical to the Jewish hierarchy of his day that he was condemned to death for them.

The Parable of the Persistent Widow (Luke 18:1-7)

Here Jesus tells a story aimed at strengthening the resolve of followers so that they not lose heart in the face of the adversity and hardships they would be sure to encounter. That he does so employing a widow is revealing of his belief that he saw in women a symbol of strength and perseverance. Certainly, their poor treatment made it so. The following verse is copied from the Gospels and needs no burnishing by the writer:

> *And he told them a parable to the effect that they ought always to pray and* ***not lose heart****. He said, "In a certain city there was a judge who neither feared God nor respected man. And there was a widow in that city who kept coming to him and saying, 'Give me justice against my adversary.' For a while he refused, but afterward he said to himself, 'Though I neither fear God nor respect man, yet because this widow keeps bothering me, I will give her justice, so that she will not beat me down by her continual coming.'"*

The Widow's Offering (Luke 21:1-4)

Jesus again uses the example of a widow to teach his followers about the essence of charity. While the Gospels contain many passages concerning the importance of charity and the need to minister to the poor, the passage that follows is perhaps one of the more poignant. It occurs during of one of Jesus' last visits to the Great Temple in Jerusalem, as he witnesses visitors giving donations to the church. The passage is entered as it appears in Luke's Gospel.

> *Jesus looked up and saw the rich putting their gifts into the offering box, and he saw a poor widow put in two small copper coins. And he said, "Truly, I tell you, this poor widow has put in more than all of them. For they all contributed out of their abundance, but she out of her poverty put in all she had to live on."*

That Jesus used the example of a widow again is revealing in that they were one of the most vulnerable groups in Jewish society. Widows didn't even have a legal right to a deceased husband's estate (sons did). However, the widow might receive a pension by her husband's family, if they were so inclined.

Conclusion

That women occupied a low station at the time of Jesus is unquestioned. They had few formal legal rights, and were forbidden to partake in commerce at any level; nor were they were permitted to have a trade. Women were consigned to the roles of homemakers or servants. Moreover, married women were considered a possession and could be summarily divorced by a written decree of their husband. (Page 69, Matthew 5:31-32) Compared to Western Society's norms, the world at that time was bleak indeed for women, which makes Jesus' positive interaction with them even more compelling.

Further, there is no recorded instance of Jesus reproaching, shaming, or stereotyping a woman; rather, his actions and words suggest he sought their liberation. His views on adultery and divorce also confirm this. (See Page 68 - Matthew 5:27-37).

Regarding the question of abortion, same-sex marriage, and gender identification, while the positions espoused by various Christian denominations differ on the subject,[39] Jesus' teachings do not directly address the matter. However, Jesus would expect each of us to show understanding, compassion, and love for every individual, regardless of whichever side of an issue they may support. Recent dictums of Pope Francis I reflect this view.[40]

Finally, no discussion on the topic would be complete without addressing the reserved role afforded women in Roman Catholic and other Christian churches, particularly given Jesus' respect for them. Firstly, there is nothing contained in any of the

Gospels that either defines a hierarchy among Jesus' followers or precludes a woman from full participation. To the contrary, Jesus repeatedly told his followers that those who sought to be first would be considered last. (See Page 113, Matthew 19:30)

However, that Jesus chose only men as his Apostles is quite understandable given the mores of a society that prohibited a woman from even speaking in public. Moreover, a woman who was seen living among men could be subject to stoning, as was described in the opening pages of this book. These norms have been prevalent throughout much of our history, and the practice of men occupying the role of the church clergy, in many faiths, has thousands of years of tradition. While modern society, and particularly women, may see this as a symbol of sexism, the Roman Catholic Church does not view the matter as such, any more than it does its canon on the celibacy of its clergy.

Interestingly, while this remains an issue to many, most Buddhist priests, and nuns are also celibate. (Buddhism is the world's fourth largest religious denomination, with over one-half billion followers.)

Common Phrases from the Gospels

Due to the power of the message they convey, many of Jesus' teachings, parables, and proverbial phrases have become part of our everyday vernacular; even the word "Gospel" itself has come to signify the veracity of something, and the name of Jesus has become a metaphor. While many of the following are well known and have been used by famous people – including Abraham Lincoln, whose "House Divided" speech still rings as a seminal moment in American history – most non-Christians do not know their origin. This narrative will attempt to provide a setting for these phases to give them context, as well discussion on what wisdom they may convey in the world of today.

All the phrases listed below are described in the narrative that follows; others attributed to followers of Jesus are noted in the last section of the book (Page 170). The wording of the phrases that follow are the most commonly known and may differ slightly from those contained in the Gospels, but their origin and meaning is unmistakable. They are entered in sequence as recorded in the cited passages.

* Various forms of the Golden Rule can be found in most, if not all, religious and spiritual-related doctrine; the most commonly used form comes down to us from Matthew's Gospel.

In addition to the above, other common practices and beliefs that have their roots in the Gospels include the oft-seen making the sign of the cross (Matthew 28:19), the crossing of one's fingers for luck or holding them behind one's back when telling a white lie,[43] and fear of the number 13, which superstition, although dating before the time of Jesus, became synonymous with bad luck, following the suicide of Judas. (See page 154)

2 Well-Known Passages

Introduction

While the entries in this book typically follow the order of the Chapters in the Gospels, the four which follow below are entered out of sequence, as they illustrate Jesus' ability to speak to significant and complex issues in simple yet memorable terms. While these passages are certainly among Jesus' most famous, the reader may find others equally compelling. In fact, Mahatma Gandhi was so taken by segments of the "Sermon on the Mount" that it is said he would recite the "Beatitudes" (Matthew 5:1-12, Page 64) every morning. The reader may also enjoy the messages contained in "Parable of the Vineyard Workers" (Matthew 20:1-16, Page 112), and the "Good Samaritan" (Luke 10:29, Page 119), among others.

Jesus' Message of Forgiveness
(John 8:7)

A famous passage that captures the essence of Jesus' ministry is taken from John Chapter 8. The scene was set in the "Preface" that opens this book. An adulterous woman is brought to Jesus by Scribes and Pharisees, who ask what is to be done with her. Jesus sees the question as a trap, since he must either affirm the law by calling for the woman to be stoned, or oppose the law and risk being charged with heresy. Since affirming the law would have gone against his messages of compassion and forgiveness, Jesus had to find a way to save the woman without violating the law or contradicting his teachings.

When questioned, Jesus did not immediately answer. Instead, he bent down and began tracing lines in the dirt and dust with a finger, as if he were alone and had nothing better on his mind. Everyone present was surprised at this and began to wonder why he was acting in such an absurd manner. Was this an act of a man possessed? Perhaps his answer was being written out, or was he simply stalling for time?[(11)]

Sensing the loss of the moment, one of the Pharisees demanded whether the woman should be stoned, as required by the law. At last Jesus straightened and looking directly at the crowd, who were staring at him in silent anticipation, answered in words that were so simple and direct that it took a few moments for their profoundness to sink in. Once the full weight of the meaning was grasped, the Temple officials who had gathered were left speechless. Amazingly, Jesus' answer neither found fault with the law nor condemned the woman!

Even more perplexing to the Pharisees, having mockingly given Jesus the authority of a learned teacher, Jesus' response left them no recourse but to free the woman, lest a judgment fall upon them! As this resignation began to show on the faces of the Pharisees and others gathered, the crowd slowly began to quietly leave in different directions, until even the Chief Priests and Pharisees walked away.

The words that Jesus used to confound those who sought his destruction have come down to us in everyday usage, and are as worthy as any ever recorded in man's long journey from antiquity to the present. It is hoped that the reader will be similarly moved by their simplicity and wisdom:

"Let he who is without sin cast the first stone" (John 8:7).

Once Jesus uttered these words, no one in the crowd dared throw a stone, as they knew the act would subject them to judgment. Doing so would be tantamount to their claiming to be sinless. These ten simple words have come down to us in our everyday vernacular and have been evoked on many occasions by Christians and non-Christians alike.

We live in a time when bad news seems to be relished by many who, egged on by a voracious media, appear only too willing to cast the first stone. Jesus asks us to give pause when we are about to act on impulse and weigh the issue carefully, mindful of our own weaknesses and transgressions, and to seek understanding and forgiveness, in lieu of anger and vengeance. This is one of Jesus' recurrent messages and one of humankind's most difficult tasks – but one we must all overcome if we are to free ourselves of the self-inflicted wounds that result when we harbor prejudice, hate, and anger.

Jesus Reconciles the Laws of God and Man
(Matthew 22:15)

That Jesus was not popular with the Jewish leaders of his time is an understatement. The Gospels contain innumerable accounts of confrontations between Jesus and the religious leaders of that time.[44] In Matthew 22:15 Jesus is publicly asked by a group of Pharisees if it is legal to pay the census tax to the Romans. Like the passage about the adulterous woman, the question is intended to trap Jesus, as the payment of taxes to the Romans was against the Jewish law, but publicly stating so could have led to his arrest on a charge of sedition against the Roman occupiers. Jesus responds by asking for a coin[45] which is used to pay this tax, and is finally given one. Holding it aloft, he asks whose likeness is on it. The Pharisees respond "Caesar," to which Jesus replies:

> ***"Then repay to Caesar what belongs to Caesar and to God what belongs to God."***

As with the situation of the adulterous woman, Jesus finds a way to respond to what would seem to be a quandary[46] – how to reconcile abeyance of the law with one's opposing moral and/or religious beliefs. The issue continues to perplex us, even as this book is written.

The question posed by the Pharisees and Jesus' response can be likened to our country's founders debate on the separation of church and state; an issue of great importance, given that many of the nation's early settlers had come to escape religious persecution. The issue was of such significance that it was addressed in the First Amendment of our Constitution, to wit:

"Congress shall make no law respecting an establishment of religion, or prohibiting the free exercise thereof."

As can be readily seen in the wording itself, the Amendment was enacted to prevent the government from passing laws that interposed upon an individual's religious beliefs. And it is equally clear that our founding fathers did not believe it necessary to protect the people from religion. Witness reference to "our Creator" in the Declaration of Independence. Even our national motto "In God We Trust" can be found on our currency.

Thomas Jefferson, one of the Constitution's framers, when asked to explain the intent of the First Amendment wrote that is was done to create a "wall of separation between the church and the state,"[47] which assuredly meant that neither should infringe on the rights of the other.

Today, one of the more contentious issues facing Americans is the growing list of court rulings that clearly infringe upon the beliefs of religious groups, particularly in the areas of contraception, abortion, marriage and gender identification. Many Americans believe that social issues such as these should be addressed through the legislature, or by amendment by the individual states, rather than by executive action or court fiat. Moreover, while many in society have accepted the contravention of laws and social mores for "conscientious objectors" and even certain Muslim practices, strongly held Christian/Judeo beliefs have not been afforded the same tolerance.

Societal issues aside, Jesus' words can also have meaning in our everyday dealings. It will come as no surprise to anyone that two sides in a negotiation typically request more and offer less, in turn, than either party views as wholly reasonable, before reaching a settlement. In fact, it is said that some cultures consider it an insult not to do so in their daily transactions. Since this practice is so prevalent that it is to be expected, there is no underlying intent to deceive. Therefore, no moral implication can be drawn. In sum, "Render unto Caesar."

The Prodigal Son

Luke 15:11-32

The Prodigal Son is certainly one of Jesus' best known and stirring parables. The story found its way into art, literature, poetry, classical and contemporary music, plays, and movies. Its message of forgiveness and redemption is at the heart of his teachings. These precepts were often repeated by Jesus, as can be seen in John 8:7 which opened this section, as well as in other parables included in this book. Because the story is so evocative, it is given here in its entirety, as it appears in Luke:

A man had two sons. The younger of them said to his father, 'Father, give me the share of the estate that falls to me.' So the father divided his wealth and gave the younger son his share of the inheritance. And not many days later, the younger son gathered everything together and went on a journey into a distant country, and there he squandered his estate with loose living. Now when he had spent everything, a severe famine occurred in that country and he began to be impoverished. So he went and hired himself out to one of the citizens of that country, and he sent him into his fields to feed swine. And he would have gladly filled his stomach with the pods that the swine were eating, and no one was giving anything to him.

But when he came to his senses, he said, 'How many of my father's hired men have more than enough bread, but I am dying here with hunger. I will get up and go to my father, and will say to him, "Father, I have sinned against heaven, and in your sight; I am no longer worthy to be called your son; make me as one of your hired men'. But while he was still a long way off, his father saw him and felt compassion for him, and ran and embraced him and kissed him. And the son said to him, 'Father, I have sinned against heaven and in your sight; I am no longer worthy to be called your son.' But the father said to his slaves, 'Quickly bring out the best robe and put it on him, and put a ring on his hand and sandals on his feet and bring the fatted calf, kill it, and let us eat and celebrate for this son of mine was dead and has come to life again; he was lost and has been found.' And they began to celebrate.

Now his older son was in the field, and when he came and approached the house, he heard music and dancing. And he summoned one of the servants and began inquiring what these things could be. And he said to him, 'Your brother has come, and your father has ***killed the fattened calf*** *because he has received him back* ***safe and sound****.' But he became angry and was not willing to go in and his father came out and began pleading with him. But he answered and said to his father, 'Look, for so many years I have been serving*

> *you and I have never neglected a command of yours and yet you have never given me a young goat, so that I might celebrate with my friends; but when this son of yours came, who has devoured your wealth with prostitutes, you killed the fatted calf for him.' And he said to him, 'Son, you have always been with me, and all that is mine is yours. But we had to celebrate and rejoice, for this brother of yours was dead and has begun to live, and was lost and has been found.'*

The powerful imagery evoked in the parable may have a special meaning to those who are estranged from other family members or old friends, whatever the cause. Undoubtedly, some readers have had experiences in their lives that led to a separation from loved ones or dear friends. Perhaps a contentious divorce or a dispute among siblings over the care and final arrangements of an elderly parent, or the handling of their estate. Jesus asks us to show compassion to those who have injured or disappointed us and to seek forgiveness when we have transgressed. There is no shame in taking the first step, as the son in this parable has done; rather, Jesus would see it as a sign of strength and goodness. There is an old saying that comes to mind here: "To err is human; to forgive divine."[48]

The Judgment of Nations

Matthew 25:31-46

Another significant passage records Jesus' words to his Apostles during the last week of his life. It was of such meaning to Leo Tolstoy that he included parts of it in one of his books.[49] In Matthew Chapter 25, Jesus prophesizes his return at the time of mankind's final judgment, which is described as time of great tribulation. Jesus tells his disciples that he will judge each person when that time arrives. Since Jesus' words are stirring, and of such meaning to all of society, the passage is given in its entirety:

> *Then the king will say to those on his right, 'Come, you who are blessed by my Father. Inherit the kingdom prepared for you from the foundation of the world.* ***For I was hungry and you gave me food,*** *I was thirsty and you gave me drink, a stranger and you welcomed me, naked and you clothed me, ill and you cared for me, in prison and you visited me. Then the righteous*[50] *will answer him and say,* ***'Lord, when did we see you hungry and feed you,*** *or thirsty and give you drink? When did we see you a stranger and welcome you, or naked and clothe you? When did we see you ill or in prison, and visit you?' And the king will say to them in reply,* ***'Amen, I say to you, whatever you did for one of these least brothers of mine, you did for me.***

Jesus' message here is a recurrent theme running through the Gospels and central to the Christian call to service to all of mankind. His words have meaning not only for his followers, but for all men and women of good will. This call in the Christian community has led to the greatest outpouring of care for the sick, poor, old and youth of any group or nation in the history of mankind. Christians, however, are not alone in this regard, as society calls all of us to respect others, no matter what their station or situation, and to provide for and protect those who are poor or powerless.

3 The Gospel According to Matthew

Introduction

While Matthew was one of Jesus' original twelve Apostles, there is a consensus among religious scholars that the Gospel was not written by him, but by a highly educated Jew and follower, based upon the Gospel's highly refined style and thorough knowledge of all aspects of Jewish law. The Gospel According to Matthew (simply "Matthew" or "Mt." hereafter) is now considered to be the second written after Mark.[51] It is accorded the honor of being the first of the four Gospels in order of their occurrence in the New Testament (The Roman Catholic version contains a total of twenty-seven collected writings), as it was once thought to be the first written.

Christian tradition tells us that the Gospel of Matthew was written early in the second century of the Christian era, some seventy years following the death of Jesus; however, some scholars believe it may have been written as early as fifty years following the death of Jesus, or somewhere between AD 80 and 90.

Matthew's Gospel encompasses virtually all that is included in the other three Gospels; including Mark's, which is relatively short (sixteen chapters) compared to Matthew's twenty-eight.

Jesus' Early Life

Matthew Chapters 1 to 3

The first three chapters in Matthew record the genealogy, birth, and early years of Jesus' life. As entered above, this narrative will focus on the years of Jesus' public ministry, which commences in Matthew Chapter 4, below. However, because Christians view the birth of Jesus as one of the central events in the history of mankind, some mention of it is warranted here.

Today, Jesus' birthday, or Christmas (literally, "Christ's Mass"), is celebrated as a national holiday throughout the western world, including, as a purely cultural celebration, in a growing number of non-Christian countries. While our calendar marks Jesus birth as December 25,[52] no one knows the actual day Jesus was born. Historians now place his birth somewhere between 6 and 3 BC. The date of December 25 was first taken in the fourth century and may have been chosen by early Christians based on the belief that Jesus was conceived on March 25 and born nine months later.

While the rituals surrounding the celebration of Christmas have changed significantly over the centuries, including being banned by Christian reform movements at times, the Christmas most of us are familiar with today was popularized by Charles Dickens' *A Christmas Carol*, which emphasized that Christmas was a time of family gatherings, merriment, charity, goodwill, and compassion. The giving of presents originated with the Gospel's telling of the baby Jesus being visited by three Magi who were wealthy and learned men from the East who brought gifts of gold, frankincense (a fragrant unguent with therapeutic properties), and myrrh (a fragrant incense).

Since the celebration of Christmas has become a symbol of one of the more contentious issues facing Americans, *i.e.*, the infringement of religion upon the rights of the individual – and *vice versa*, it is hoped that the perspective of Jesus as a great teacher and social reformer, as set forth in this writing, will help ameliorate the divisiveness that accompanies this national holiday; particularly given the honor accorded to one of his ardent followers who was among America's greatest social reformers, the Reverend Doctor Martin Luther King, Jr.

While all fair-minded people can understand the legitimate concern for the public display of the religious aspects of the holiday, the hostility that now seems to greet even the words "Merry Christmas" leave many Christians perplexed, particularly given that the over-the-top commercialization and many non-Christian traditions that now accompany it – including holiday lighting, Christmas Trees, songs like *Jingle Bells* and *White Christmas*, the Yule log, mistletoe, holly, Frosty, Rudolph, and the Grinch, to name a few.

These temporal symbols have all but rendered Christmas a secular event. Ironically, since more than a few historians now believe the early church may have chosen the date to co-opt the numerous pagan celebrations that took place at that time of year, the celebration of Christmas on December 25 may in fact be secular in origin.[53]

That Christmas has more and more become a cultural holiday is undeniable; however, the central meaning to Christians (whatever the actual date of Jesus' birth) remains one of peace on earth and goodwill to men. Certainly no one can take issue with these precepts.

Jesus Begins His Public Ministry

Matthew 4:1-4

Jesus began his public ministry around the age of thirty, and it lasted only a few years. The Gospels tell us that Jesus spent his formative years working as a carpenter, which was the occupation of his father, Joseph. Matthew Chapter 4 commences with the account of Jesus fasting in the desert for forty days and nights, followed by a journey to Galilee, where he called on his Apostles to join him in his mission. The number 40 itself is significant throughout the Old and New Testaments and generally occurs in connection with judgment and testing. Genesis tells us that the great Flood and testing of Noah occurred during forty days and nights of continuous rain. Exodus tells us the children of Israel wandered in the desert for forty years before reaching the Promised Land. Luke tells us that Jesus also visited his Apostles over a period of forty days following his death.

Matthew writes that as the forty days of fasting came to an end, the devil came to Jesus and tested his will, saying that if he were the son of God he could compel rocks to become loaves of bread. Jesus' response gave rise to a common phase that has come down to us through the Gospels: "Man does not live by bread alone"; the passage comes to us from Matthew 4:4, which reads:

> *The Tempter approached and said to him, 'If you are the Son of God, command that these stones become loaves of bread." He said in reply, "It is written,* ***One does not live by bread alone,*** *but by every word that comes forth from the mouth of God."*

Jesus is clearly setting the tone for his ministry in this passage and its underlying message that there are more important things in life than one's physical well-being. Jesus' fast also serves to test his will and endurance – which he will need for the trials he is to face during his public ministry. His actions remind us that we too must have discipline and make sacrifices to achieve our goals. This denial of self is central to the beliefs of many faiths and belief systems.

Jesus Calls His Apostles

Matthew 4:18-22

Following the forty days of fasting, Jesus went to the neighboring area of Galilee to seek those who would become his Apostles. Matthew 4:12-22 tells us of how this came about:

> *As he was walking by the Sea of Galilee, he saw two brothers, Simon who is called Peter, and his brother Andrew, casting a net into the sea; they were fishermen. He said to them, 'Come after me, and I will make you* ***fishers of men.*** *' At once they left their nets and followed him. He walked along from there and saw two other brothers, James, the son of Zebedee, and his brother John. They were in a boat, with their father Zebedee, mending their nets. He called them, and immediately they left their boat and their father and followed him.*

The phrase "fishers of men"[54] is perhaps one of the more familiar metaphors that have come down to us. It can be found in literature (and art), including Geoffrey Chaucer's *Summoner's Tale*, Lord Byron's *Don Juan*, Alfred Tennyson's *Harold*, James Joyce's *A Portrait of the Artist as a Young Man*, and G. K. Chesterton's *The Innocence of Father Brown*.

Matthew tells us that Jesus then went throughout Galilee with his disciples, teaching in the synagogues and healing the sick. As he went, his fame spread throughout Judea and Syria, and great crowds began to follow him.

4 The Sermon on the Mount

Matthew Chapter 5

Introduction

Matthew Chapters 5, 6, and 7

Shortly after beginning his public ministry Jesus began to draw crowds as he preached throughout Judea. One day when walking near the Sea of Galilee Jesus saw that the size of the crowd that was following him was growing into the thousands and he went to the side of a mountain (Luke identifies it as a plain) so that all might see him. He began to preach to them in what has come to be known as the "Sermon on the Mount." This sermon is perhaps the best known of Jesus' discourses and covers a wide range of moral, ethical and philosophical teachings, including anger, adultery, divorce, taking oaths, retaliation, charity, loving one's enemies, and others. At nearly two thousand words, the sermon is by far Jesus' longest continuous discourse in the Gospels, covering all of Matthew Chapters 5, 6, and 7. Jesus' Sermon on the Mount has inspired many throughout history, including both Mahatma Gandhi[55] and Martin Luther King Jr.,[56] whose nonviolent non-cooperative protest movements were framed in Matthew 5:38-42, which follows below.

Because so much of Jesus' message to mankind is contained within the Sermon on the Mount, it is necessary to give it full voice for anyone who wishes to learn what Jesus has to say to them. Much of the sermon is therefore summarized in the following along with, it is hoped, relative commentary on where the passages have inspired mankind and what those words may mean to us in today's world.

"The Beatitudes"
(Matthew 5:1-12)

Jesus' Sermon on the Mount commences with what Christians refer to as the "Beatitudes" (from the Latin word "happiness"). Because of its brevity, it is entered completely as it appears in Matthew. As noted earlier, Mahatma Gandhi was a great admirer of Jesus and was so taken by the beauty and meaning of the Beatitudes that it is said that he recited them as part of his morning prayers. The Beatitudes consist of nine blessings, each proverb-like, that have their origins in the Old Testament, and are composed of two elements – the circumstance and the blessing:

> *Blessed are the poor in spirit,* **for theirs is the kingdom of heaven.*
>
> *Blessed are they who mourn, for they will be comforted.*
>
> *Blessed are the meek, for they will inherit the land.*
>
> *Blessed are they who hunger and thirst for righteousness, for they will be satisfied.*
>
> *Blessed are the merciful, for they will be shown mercy.*
>
> *Blessed are the clean of heart, for they will see God.*
>
> *Blessed are the peacemakers, for they will be called children of God.*
>
> *Blessed are they who are persecuted for the sake of*

---

* The word "poor" (from the Hebrew *anawim*), as used by Jesus, was taken from the Old Testament and referred to those who are without material possessions but whose confidence is in God.

righteousness, for theirs is the kingdom of heaven.

Blessed are you when they insult you and persecute you and utter every kind of evil against you [falsely] because of me... Rejoice and be glad, for your reward will be great in heaven. Thus they persecuted the prophets who were before you. *

The Beatitudes represent the core of Jesus' teachings and were intended as a lesson of the virtues one must embody to attain spiritual peace. Their message of humility, generosity, love, kindness, self-control, temperance, and fortitude represent the antithesis of the seven deadly sins of pride, greed, envy, anger, lust, gluttony, and sloth. While they may appear naïve and unattainable in modern society, many appear in one form or other in many of the world's great religions, including Islam, Hinduism, and Buddhism, and reflect the near universal concept of surrender of the self as the highest spiritual ideal.

Jesus Charges His Disciples
Matthew 5:13-16

Here Jesus tells his disciples that they are like the *"salt of the earth"* and the *"light of the world."*† In the time of Jesus salt was extremely important and, in places where it was scarce, it was even used as currency. In addition to being essential nutritionally, salt was, and continues to be, used to flavor, purify, and preserve food. In this passage Jesus inspires his followers to

---

* Jesus is both cautioning and strengthening the resolve of those who would follow, as they will be persecuted for their dedication to him, which indeed they were.

† Jesus' words call to mind something once said by Buddha: "Thousands of candles can be lighted from a single candle, and the life of the candle will not be shortened."

persevere in their efforts to free the world from moral corruption by their words and deeds, and to become a beacon of goodness for all to see. He admonishes them that should they lose their passion, they will become like flavorless salt and their words will be dim as a light under a basket.

> *"You are the* ***salt of the earth.*** *But if salt loses its taste, with what can it be seasoned? It is no longer good for anything but to be thrown out and trampled underfoot."*
>
> ***"You are the light of the world . . .*** *your light must shine before others, that they may see your good deeds and glorify your heavenly Father."*

There is a parallel to be seen here in modern society's quest for the ever-increasing satisfaction of the individual's senses, to the point where normal living becomes dull and unfulfilling. When that happens the simple everyday things we may have enjoyed during an earlier time are lost seemingly without the possibility of recovery; the flavor of life is gone.

However, Jesus does offer those who yearn to recover that earlier sense of optimism and *joie de vivre* a way to rediscover that connection. It may have been expressed best in a quote attributed to Mahatma Gandhi "The best way to find ourselves is in the service of others."

Jesus Came to Fulfill the Law of the Prophets
Matthew 5:17-19

Jesus assures his followers that he did not come to replace the Mosaic law,[57] but rather to complete it. While he instructed his disciples to obey the law, he also advocated that the people seek a higher righteousness than he saw in the examples of the Scribes, Pharisees, and High Priests of that time.

> *"Do not think that I have come to abolish the law or the*

> *prophets. I have come not to abolish but to fulfill . . . whoever breaks one of the least of these commandments and teaches others to do so will be called least in the kingdom of heaven . . . I tell you, unless your righteousness surpasses that of the scribes and Pharisees, you will not enter into the kingdom of heaven."*

Unfortunately, while Jesus' words were directed at the religious leaders of his day, they have as much meaning today as when he invoked them. Speaking only of Christianity, and given the many crimes that have been committed in Jesus' name over the centuries since his death, it is no wonder many have lost respect for the institutions that are considered part of "His" Church.

More recently, the abuse of children by clergy has led to further disparagement of Jesus' message. Regrettably, those who committed these heinous acts did so in the face of what Jesus saw as the most damning of all the sins, the harming of a child (Matthew 18:6-9, See Page 107). Hopefully, the reader can set aside any negative feelings about Christian churches and clergy, and simply consider Jesus' message.

Jesus Teaches About Anger

Matthew 5:21-22

Here Jesus tells the gathered crowd to contain their anger toward others who may have wronged them, lest they be subject to the same judgment they themselves have made. Jesus extends this message to include acts of retaliation and the necessity to love one's enemies, as entered in the passages which follow below (Matthew 5:38-43, See Page 71). Jesus' message here is as relevant today as it was when first spoken:

> *"You have heard that it was said to your ancestors 'You shall not kill; and whoever kills will be liable to*

> *judgment.' **But I say to you, whoever is angry with his brother will be liable to judgment.**"*

The reader may have heard the saying "curse the act and not the person." If we do this, we can allow for human frailty, while still condemning the deed. There is also an old saying regarding anger (and hate): "Anger is like a flame; it burns the holder more than the object it seeks to consume."

The reader may also be familiar with the saying "whom the gods wish to destroy, they first make mad." (spoken by Prometheus in the poem *The Masque of Pandora* by Henry W. Longfellow)

Jesus Talks About Adultery
Matthew 5:27-28

While the Ten Commandments forbid the coveting of a neighbor's wife, Jesus tells the crowd that a married man who lusts after *any* woman has already committed adultery in his heart, and that it would be better to lose an eye than commit that sin. While Jesus' words here are clearly directed at the nature of men,* they also affirm the respect he had towards women.

> *"You have heard that it was said 'You shall not commit adultery. But I say to you, everyone who looks at a woman with lust has already committed adultery with her in his heart."*

While Jesus' words seem out of touch in today's liberated society, can anyone find fault in his admonishment? We have all

---

* In Jesus' time, women were considered a husband's property, and could be stoned for committing adultery; but not so with men. It is therefore not surprising that this passage was directed towards men.

known or have heard of marriages that have been broken because one partner or the other sought gratification outside their marriage. How many would be honest enough to later admit that doing so was a mistake, perhaps the greatest they ever made?

Jesus Talks About Divorce
Matthew 5:31-32

Here Jesus uses strong words to condemn divorce, which he later reaffirms when confronted by Pharisees who considered this teaching heretical (Matthew 19:1-12, Page 109). Interestingly, while Jesus' main issue here was with the faithfulness of men to the marital vows, it can readily be viewed as support for the rights of the wife, since Mosaic law allowed a man to divorce his wife by simply delivering a letter to the local scribe.

> *"It was also said, 'Whoever divorces his wife must give her a bill of divorce. But I say to you, whoever divorces his wife (unless the marriage is unlawful)* causes her to commit adultery, and whoever marries a divorced woman commits adultery.* [58]

Jesus' admonition here is likely to be greeted with derision by many and seen as unattainable by others. While we all know that some marriages are better off dissolved, far too many divorces are the result of egocentricity; witness the number of multiple marriages/divorces which are now commonplace. It appears that many now look upon marriage as just another form of business

---

* While the Roman Catholic Church considers divorce wrongful, it has accepted that "invalid" marriages can be annulled. In recent years, based on a broader reading of this verse and others, the grounds for annulment have been expanded. Further, many of the most staunchly Christian nations, including Italy, have legalized divorce.

contract, with legal escape clauses known as a "pre-nuptial agreement," rather than a commitment to the vows that were taken when a couple married. Not surprisingly, studies consistently show that the divorce rate is significantly lower when couples practice the principles that Jesus espouses.

Jesus Tells Us Not to Take Oaths
Matthew 5:33-37

Jesus' words here are striking, given the lack of forthrightness that exists in the world today. We truly reside in a society of lies, half-truths, and ambiguity. Jesus addresses this, as follows:

> *"Again you have heard that it was said to your ancestors, 'Do not take a false oath . . . But I say to you, do not swear at all; not by heaven, for it is God's throne; nor by the earth, for it is his footstool . . . Do not swear by your head, for you cannot make a single hair white or black.* ***Let your 'Yes' mean 'Yes,' and your 'No' mean 'No.' Anything more is from the evil one."***

Jesus' simple yet compelling words here are a lesson for all of society. We see deceitfulness everywhere, which is why there are truth-in-lending and advertising laws and why most now question the integrity of our media, politicians, and even our legal, medical, educational, and religious systems.

Even "sworn" testimony now only rests with the candor that the threat of being prosecuted for false statements can muster. How many times have we seen someone swear to tell the "whole truth," only to assert their right under the Fifth Amendment, not to do so? Worse still, many only see the "truth" to the extent that it fits within preconceived parameters of their socioeconomic belief system, which is aided by a new medical expert, the "spin doctor," who specializes in explaining how the painfully obvious is neither.

While many readers will see Jesus' message here as naïve and unattainable in today's world, if each of us is sincere in the desire to promote a better world, we must hold ourselves and others to a higher standard, and become a beacon of truth. As Saint Francis of Assisi once said, "All the darkness in the world cannot extinguish the light of a single candle."

Jesus Talks About Retaliation
Matthew 5:38-42

Jesus' words here are truly historic. Both Mahatma Gandhi and Martin Luther King Jr.'s nonviolent, non-cooperative protest movements were inspired by them. No one can add anything to that, and so they are given verbatim.

> *"You have heard that it was said, 'An eye for an eye and a tooth for a tooth.'* But I say to you, offer no resistance to one who is evil.* ***When someone strikes you on (your) right cheek, turn the other one to him as well."***

There is a scene in the wonderful movie *Gandhi* where Mahatma Gandhi (Ben Kingsley) talks to a reporter about the nature of the movement he was leading at the time. He tells the reporter that Jesus' teaching that one should turn a cheek when struck by an oppressor and offer the other defines the movement, and that the submission of the people to the British harsh treatment is anything but passive; rather he saw it as a powerful act and statement that elevated the person who was struck, while diminishing the other. Indeed, testimony to the power of this principle was demonstrated in the termination of nearly 200

---

* The quote is taken from the Old Testament, Ex. 21:24

years of British rule in India, as well as by the results of the 1960's Civil Rights Movement in the United States.

Love Your Enemies

Matthew 5:43-47

Virtually all of us would find it impossible to love those who would harm us or our loved ones. Jesus clearly is *not* telling us to remain passive in the face of evil. He is asking us to remember we are all members of the human family. Jesus elevates the Golden Rule when he says the following:

> *"You have heard that it was said, 'You shall love your neighbor and hate your enemy. But I say to you,* ***love your enemies, and pray for those who persecute you,*** *that you may be children of your heavenly Father,* ***for he makes his sun rise on the bad and the good, and causes rain to fall on the just and the unjust. For if you love those who love you, what recompense will you have?*** *So be perfect,*[59] *just as your heavenly Father is perfect."*

One of humanity's great paradoxes occurs when men in battle against sworn "enemies" can, in the passage of time, find their hatred has turned to compassion, with the realization that their enemies were men much like themselves, who suffered, as well. This was poignantly brought home in the life story of Louis Zamperini, which was the subject of a best-selling book and movie.[60] The story shows that Zamperini found peace through a spiritual awakening, after years of inner turmoil and drinking problems.

Amazingly, this spiritual rebirth allowed him to forgive a sadistic war prison guard nicknamed "the Bird" (Mutsuhiro Watanabe), who had brutalized him. When discovered alive in 1998, Watanabe, who had evaded capture as a war criminal, expressed no remorse and even refused to see Zamperini. Despite this,

Zamperini wrote Watanabe a letter expressing his forgiveness and love!

Martin Luther King Jr. may have said it best: "Darkness cannot overcome darkness – only light can do that. Hate cannot overcome hate – only love can do that."[61]

5 The Sermon on the Mount – Continued

Matthew Chapter 6

Jesus Talks About Charity

Matthew 6:1-4

There are many passages in the Gospels that witness Jesus' message of charity. Here, Jesus gives us one of the more evocative ones, telling us that charity should be done for its own sake, and not for the recognition of the generosity of the giver. The passage entered directly below, and those that follow in Matthew Chapter 6 are among the most seminal of Jesus' messages.

> *"Take care not to perform righteous deeds in order that people may see them; otherwise, you will have no recompense from your heavenly Father. When you give alms, do not blow a trumpet before you ... to win the praise of others. Amen, I say to you, they have received their reward. But when you give alms,* ***do not let your left hand know what your right is doing,*** *so that your almsgiving may be secret. And your Father who sees in secret will repay you."*

Jesus' teaching here calls to mind those who wish to be "anonymous donors." Contrasting this is society's apparent need to seek out and label all do-gooders as "heroes." Jesus does not see such action as remarkable, at all. His words should also remind us that giving is its own reward, and the giver is often more grateful than the receiver, since it allows them to share their prosperity. Anyone who has taken the time and effort to learn to play a musical instrument, or to become a gourmet cook, will tell you that the real enjoyment comes in witnessing the fruits of the labors enjoyed by others. So it is with acts of charity.

There is also a corollary to this passage in Luke 14:12-14, wherein Jesus again talks of charity in the "Parable of Invited Guests and Host" (Luke 14:7-14, Page 124).

Jesus Talks About Prayer

Matthew 6:5-8

Jesus' Sermon on the Mount continues with Jesus telling his followers how to pray.

> *"When you pray . . . go to your inner room, close the door, and pray to your Father in secret. And your Father who sees in secret will repay you. In praying, do not babble like the pagans, who think that they will be heard because of their many words ... Your Father knows what you need before you ask him."*

The recording of Jesus' words here is not intended to motivate anyone to pray; however, since prayer was such an integral part of his ministry,[62] anyone seeking an understanding of Jesus should consider his words on prayer. Moreover, Jesus' call to prayer is by no means unique; prayer, and its handmaiden meditation, is universal to all faiths. Many have witnessed scenes of Jews praying at the Wailing Wall in Jerusalem, or devout Muslims directing their daily prayers to Mecca, or a Catholic's simple act of making the Sign of the Cross. Similar rituals are practiced in virtually all spiritual followings, including Hinduism, Shintoism, Buddhism and many others. In fact, I have read that a Zen Buddhist Monk's entire life is spent in prayer and meditation.[63]

Gandhi likened prayer to "the key of the morning and the bolt at night." Gandhi also said of prayer "Prayer is not asking. It is a longing of the soul. It is daily admission of one's weakness."[64]

And the practice of prayer and meditation does not require invoking a divinity. Those who seek peace through quiet meditation understand this well. And are not many of our inner desires a prayer, as is the act of calling on some inner source of strength, or the seeking of the intervention of something beyond us, a form of prayer as well? The success of all 12-step and other similar self-help programs resides in the acceptance of a higher power,[65] which can be whatever an individual sees as greater than the self.

Finally, we all have admired and loved people who are no longer with us; and at times we may have even wondered what advice they might give when we are confronted with problems in our lives. Many may have even talked to that person in the quiet of their own hearts, in the hope that that person's wisdom would come to them. When that voice does come, we find comfort, even if we know that the answer was inside of us all along, waiting to be called out in the name of someone perhaps more trusted than ourselves. When we do this, are we not praying? Christians believe that the model Jesus has given mankind through his teachings can provide that inner voice of wisdom and peace. In effect, simply asking "What would Jesus do in this circumstance?" is sufficient for them to receive an unassailable response in most circumstances.

"The Lord's Prayer" – The Underlying Message

Matthew 6:9-15

There are two remarkable things about the best-known and most-recited prayer in Christendom – its brevity and simplicity. It is only five lines long and contains but fifty-five words. While members of other faiths, or those who have none, may question the purpose of its inclusion here, Jesus' words are as famous as any uttered in his lifetime and signal a substantive shift in what Jesus wanted his followers to believe in regard to man's relationship with his Creator. This will be discussed following the prayer.

Also worthy of note is the fact that the prayer is not about Jesus; rather, it is a collection of seven petitions directed to his father, who is the same whether we call him God, Allah (Aramaic for "God"), Jehovah, Yahweh, or higher power. Jesus' words were spoken in response to an entreaty from a large crowd that had gathered to hear him speak. When asked by the people how they should pray, he turned and looking up, raised his arms and called upon their father to hear the supplications of the gathered crowd, saying:

> *"Our Father, who art in heaven, hallowed be thy name,*
>
> *Thy kingdom come, Thy will be done, on earth as it is in heaven.*
>
> *Give us this day our daily bread and forgive us our trespasses, as we forgive those who trespass against us.*
>
> *And lead us not into temptation, but deliver us from evil."* [66]

Catholics (after a short invocation) and those of other Christian denominations end the Lord's Prayer with the following words:

> *For Thine is the Kingdom, the power and glory forever, Amen.*

The truly remarkable thing about the prayer lies in the fact that the word "Father," as used by Jesus, was translated from the Latin word *Pater*, which was translated from Jesus' native Aramaic term *Abba*. In Jesus' time, *Abba* was a term of love and trust one expressed when referring to the head of one's family. Jesus referred to God as *Abba* throughout his ministry, indicating his belief that mankind shared a personal relationship with their creator. This represented a departure from the Old Testament, wherein God is more often a fearful, unapproachable, all-powerful being, while merciful, capable of jealousy, anger, and even vengeance. Muslims view Allah as an all-powerful and merciful being, whom sinners should fear, as well.*

Self-Sacrifice – Fasting

Matthew 6:16-18

Self-sacrifice, in the form of fasting, is an important part of the rituals practiced by virtually all spiritual and religious followings. Eastern rites consider fasting a means of cleansing the mind and body. Muslims do so during Ramadan, Christians during Lent, and Jews during Yom Kippur. Jesus is said to have fasted for forty days and nights and tells us to approach fasting as one does prayer, inconspicuously. Matthew records his words as follows:

> *"When you fast, do not look gloomy like the hypocrites. They neglect their appearance, so that they may appear to others to be fasting. Amen, I say to you, they have received their reward. But when you fast, anoint your head and wash your face, so that you may not appear to be fasting, except to your Father who is hidden. And your Father who sees what is hidden will repay you."*

---

* "Allah had called upon all people in every era to fear Him. Allah says: 'And We had enjoined upon those who were given the Scripture before – as well as yourselves – to fear Allah.'" (Sûrah al-Nisâ' : 131)

Jesus' words here remind us that those who seek to bring attention to their piety have already lost it.

Jesus Talks About Worldly Possessions
Matthew 6:19-34

Jesus' words here remind us of the transience of wealth and the futility of a life spent in acquiring it over all other human endeavors. Jesus exhorts us to store our "treasure" in heaven – which can be viewed as a metaphor for leading a life that is based on recognizing the need to share one's prosperity with those less fortunate. Jesus' words in the passages that follow directly are some of the most compelling that have come down to us in everyday usage from the Gospels; Matthew records them as follows:

> *"Do not store up for yourselves treasures on earth, where moth and decay destroy, and thieves break in and steal. But store up treasures in heaven, where neither moth nor decay destroys, nor thieves break in and steal.* ***For where your treasure is, there also will your heart be."***
>
> ***"No one can serve two masters****. He will either hate one and love the other, or be devoted to one and despise the other. You cannot serve God and mammon."**
>
> *"Therefore I tell you, do not worry about your life, what you will eat [or drink], or about your body, what you will wear. Is not life more than food and the body more than clothing? Can any of you by worrying add a single moment to your life-span?*
>
> *Seek first the kingdom [of God] and his righteousness, and all these things will be given you besides. Do not worry about tomorrow; tomorrow will take care of itself.* ***Sufficient for a day is its own evil."***[67]

The philosophy expounded by Jesus here has found its way into

---

* From the Aramaic word *Mamon*, meaning "money" or "riches."

literature, art, music, and movies. Saint Francis of Assisi founded the Franciscan order embraced by Pope Francis 1, based on this and similar passages. Entry into the order requires the taking vows of poverty, chastity, and obedience.

Jesus' words here contrast with what may be one of society's greatest ills, the pursuit of personal wealth and power without concern for one's fellow man or the environment. Hand-in-hand with this is the belief that one's wealth and/or station (even when inherited) gives rise to feelings of superiority over the less fortunate.

6 The Sermon on the Mount Concludes

Matthew Chapter 7

Jesus Talks about Judging Others
Matthew 7:1-4

As with many of Jesus' teachings in the Sermon on the Mount, his words here have become part of the adages that have come down to us from the Gospels. So too is the entreaty for us to examine our own behavior before condemning others. Matthew records Jesus' words as follows:

> *"**Stop judging, that you may not be judged.** For as you judge, so will you be judged, and the measure with which you measure will be measured out to you. Why do you notice the splinter in your brother's eye, but do not perceive the wooden beam in your own eye? You hypocrite, **remove the wooden beam from your eye first; then you will see clearly to remove the splinter from your brother's eye.**"*

This is another of the more difficult teachings of Jesus to put into practice, particularly since we must always weigh the words and actions of those who may affect our lives and that of others. That is why society has laws and regulations and a system of enforcing them. However, Jesus is not asking us to turn a blind eye to those whose conduct could result in negative consequences to others. In fact, in Matthew 18:15-20 (See Page 108).

Jesus advises his disciples on how to treat transgressors, instructing them to judge offenders following a hearing by their peers.

Jesus' message here is reminiscent of a story Leo F. Buscaglia tells of a person driving on a narrow, winding mountain road who is passed by a motorist who shouts out the word "Pig!" as he drives by. The insulted driver responds with a few expletives and a gesture that most of us have witnessed in similar situations, only to crash into a very large pig as he rounds a blind curve.[68]

Who Will Receive Jesus' Message?
Matthew 7:5-6

Here Jesus reminds his followers not to proclaim his words in the face of ridicule and dismissal. He refers to his teachings as "pearls," which some believe popularized the phrase "pearls of wisdom." Matthew records Jesus' words as follows:

> *"Do not give what is holy to dogs, or* ***throw your pearls before swine,*** ** lest they trample them underfoot, and turn and tear you to pieces."*

While Jesus' words were aimed at those who would reject his message of peace and forgiveness, most of us are turned off by any attempt to have another's beliefs imposed on us. Today, given that so much information is at our fingertips, proselytizing one's beliefs is considered inappropriate and even bad manners by most. However, in Jesus' time, virtually all messages were disseminated orally; the only way for anyone to hear the "good

---

* Jews in Jesus' time showed their contempt for nonbelievers by referring to them as dogs and swine; pigs being an animal deplored in Jewish and Muslim traditions.

news" was by someone giving witness to it.

There is a 12-step tradition which addresses this in a way most religious and advocacy zealots would do good to practice. Instead of actively seeking adherents, it shuns publicity; its slogan in this regard states that the program is one of "attraction" rather than "promotion." Hopefully, the author has not crossed that line.

Are Prayers Answered?

Matthew 7:7-11

Jesus speaks about the power of prayer in terms that have found wide usage beyond their initial objective of fostering reliance on God. Jesus' call for his followers to pray is repeated throughout the Gospels and is discussed in some detail, above. Matthew records Jesus' words as follows:

> *"**Ask and it will be given to you; seek and you will find; knock and the door will be opened to you**. For everyone who asks, receives; and the one who seeks, finds; and to the one who knocks, the door will be opened. Which one of you would hand his son a stone when he asks for a loaf of bread. . . . If you then, who are wicked, know how to give good gifts to your children, how much more will your heavenly Father give good things to those who ask him."*

In truth, many do not believe in the power of prayer. We are quick to curse bad luck and marvel when good luck finds us, and see them as the two sides of the same coin. Despite this, who among us whose life is threatened by illness or calamity, or whose loved ones are similarly challenged, has not turned to the intervention of some power beyond our comprehension?

For many Christians, the prayer they believe will always be answered is one that seeks the inner strength to sustain them through life's trials.*

"The Golden Rule"
Matthew 7:12

While the concept of the Golden Rule is common to most cultures, the form that most of us are familiar with comes from Matthew's Gospel.

> ***"Do to others whatever you would have them do to you. This is the law of the prophets."***

The universality of this saying requires no further comment, except to suggest that its principle would also require that we also regard others as we would have them regard us.

The Gate to Salvation is Narrow
Matthew 7:13-14

Whether we believe in a heaven, or a life hereafter, humanity implores us to lead a virtuous life. Here, Jesus acknowledges the difficulty of doing so as he reminds us that the gate for those who seek righteousness is narrow, while the gate and road of perdition is wide. The tenth-century Christian Abbé Saint Bernard of Clairvaux gave us a parallel: "The road to hell is paved with good intentions." Jesus expresses this as follows:

> *"Enter through the narrow gate; for the gate is wide and the road broad that leads to destruction and those*

---

* Interestingly, Jews appear to share this belief, as expressed by Rabbi Harold Kushner during an on-air interview with Rabbi Peter J. Rubinstein (92Y on *NYCLife* – air date March 30, 2016). Rabbi Kushner recounted a story of a young man who had come to him to ask why God had not answered his prayers. The Rabbi answered (paraphrasing) "Do you think God is Santa Claus?" The Rabbi's comments confirmed that, like Christians, Jews believe that while God responds to prayers, the only one that we can be certain he answers is the one that asks for the strength to bear life's burdens.

> *who enter through it are many. How narrow the gate and constricted the road that leads to life. And those who find it are few."*

Jesus again reminds us how difficult it is to lead a righteous life; in Matthew 19:16-24 below (Page 111), Jesus tells his followers that it is easier for a camel to pass through the eye of a needle, than for a rich man to enter heaven.

Jesus Warns of False Prophets
Matthew 7:15-20

Jesus' words here have given rise to other common expressions we hear today. He uses these terms to warn his followers of false prophets who will come bearing promises of peace and prosperity. The opening words of the passage have come to signify anyone who tries to represent themselves as something they are not, usually for their own benefit.

> ***"Beware of false prophets, who come to you in sheep's clothing, but underneath are ravenous wolves.*** *By their fruits you will know them … A good tree cannot bear bad fruit, nor can a rotten tree bear good fruit…* ***by their fruits you will know them."***

Unfortunately, the world has always abounded in "false prophets," including some who seek to use Jesus' teachings for personal gain. Jesus tells us that we can judge the sincerity of those who seek to use his name by the "fruits they bear."

While Christianity has borne bitter fruits on too many occasions, those who have faithfully followed Jesus teachings can boast many good fruits, from world leaders to theologians whose writings have influenced Western culture, to respected authors and individuals, to leaders in Christian Churches, such the Reverend Billy Graham, Martin Luther King Jr., and more recently,

Mother Teresa of Calcutta and Pope Francis I.

Who Are the True Disciples?

Matthew 7:21

Jesus continues his discourse on prophets, telling them that the only true disciples are those who do the will of God.

> *"Not everyone who says to me, '**Lord, Lord,**' will enter the kingdom of heaven, but only the one who does the will of my Father in heaven."*

As he does throughout the Gospels, Jesus shows his humility by his deference to his Father in heaven, and repeatedly admonishes his followers to do the same. *"Thy will, not mine."* Unfortunately, some believe that knowledge of the scriptures constitutes proof of their virtuousness, and that citing specific passages on various subjects places them on a high moral ground. However, "lording" such knowledge to prove their piety is far from what Jesus intended.

Build Your Spiritual Houses on Solid Ground

Matthew 7:24-25

Foreshadowing his words to his first Apostle, Peter, *"You are the rock upon which I will build my church,"* (Mt. 16:13-19, See Page 102) Jesus uses the example of building upon solid ground as a metaphor for the church he envisions for his followers. Jesus likens those who harken to his words as one who would build their spiritual houses on rock. Matthew records them as follows:

> *"Everyone who listens to these words of mine and acts on them will be like **a wise man who built his house on rock**. The rain fell, the floods came, and the winds blew and buffeted the house. But it did not collapse; it had been set solidly on rock."*

What is interesting here is Jesus' use of the word "rock," which led to his Apostle Simon being called Peter from the Greek word for rock, *petros*. Today's engineers know that the tallest and most stable buildings are built upon solid rock; it was not a common practice in the time of Jesus. It appears that he fully expected his ministry to remain as long as man survived.

The Sermon on the Mount Concludes

Matthew 7:28-29

The last paragraphs of the Sermon on the Mount contain the following words:

> *"When Jesus finished these words,* ***the crowds were astonished at his teaching,*** *for he taught them as one having authority."*

Most of the people who heard Jesus' Sermon on the Mount knew little of him before that time. The reaction of the crowd attests to their amazement that someone so young could speak with such wisdom and passion. Indeed, the impact of his words were such that they are still repeated every day by millions, many of whom do not know they are doing so.

Other Discourses in Matthew

Matthew's Gospel includes others of Jesus' great public discourses in his Gospel, which are entered below and summarized here:

Matthew 10:1-40 (Page 91). Jesus charges his Apostles to undertake his mission.

Matthew 11:2-19 (Page 93) Jesus talks to a crowd about John the Baptist, who, as scholars of antiquity have confirmed, was put to death by Herod Antipas.

Matthew 13:1-53 (Page 95) Jesus explains to a gathering and

his disciples why his message is in parables and gives seven, one of which is entered below.

Matthew 19:1-30 ((Pages 109 to 112) Jesus preaches to a crowd on various subjects, including how difficult it is for a rich man to enter heaven

Matthew 26:26-30 (Page 150) This passage contains the words Jesus spoke to his Apostles during the "Last Supper," the remembrance of which is celebrated by Christians as the most solemn part of their Mass.

7 Matthew Chapters 8 to 15

Introduction

When Jesus finished the Sermon on the Mount he went down to the fishing village of Capernaum and was followed by a great crowd, including a Roman Centurion, who asked Jesus to heal his servant (See Page 40). As his fame grew he began to be questioned by the Jewish religious leaders of the day, because his message and actions were seen as radical and a threat to their authority. While many miracles are described in Matthew 8 to 15, only those which contain common expressions entered at pages 47 and 48 will be recounted, as they are needed to add context and meaning to them.

Those Who Follow the Son of Man Will Have No Rest

Matthew 8:18-20

In this passage, Jesus is about to leave the crowd that has been following him, when a Scribe[69] approaches and says he wants to join him. Jesus warns the scribe that doing so would result in his becoming an outcast, as he and his disciples would become.

The passage reads as follows:

> *When Jesus saw a crowd around him, he gave orders to cross to the other side.* A scribe approached and said to him, "Teacher, I will follow you wherever you go."*

---

* Referring to the Sea of Galilee.

> *Jesus answered him, **"Foxes have dens and birds of the sky have nests, but the Son of Man**[70] **has nowhere to rest his head."***

Obviously, Jesus was not deterred by this realization. However, while Jesus' warning was intended for all who would follow him, he also promised to give "rest" to them as well. (Matthew 11:28, Page 93).

The Calling of Matthew, a Tax Collector, is Questioned

Matthew 9:9-13

Here Jesus' calling of Matthew is questioned by many, including the Pharisees, since tax collectors were considered sinners who were despised and shunned by the populous and, no doubt, the Romans as well – true pariahs. When Jesus is asked why he consorted with tax collectors he replied:

> ***"Those who are well do not need a physician, but the sick do.*** *Go and learn the meaning of the words,* ***'I desire mercy, not sacrifice.'*** I did not come to call the righteous but sinners."*

There is an interesting parallel here between Jesus calling on someone shunned by society and the rise of the 12-step programs that have become the saving grace for many who are cursed with addictions. The most striking thing about these programs is that they are founded on the principle that the only sure way to remain clean and sober is to help a fellow addict remain so! A

---

* Jesus answered those who questioned him by quoting scripture, Hos. 6:6, which includes the words in boldface included here and continues "and the knowledge of God rather than burnt offerings." The term "sacrifice" above is clearly referring to the ritual of seeking God's favor or pardon, which Jesus sees as less pleasing to God than the quality of mercy.

true paradox when we consider that society tells us that those with addictions should avoid others with the same condition.

The Compassion of Jesus

Matthew 9:35-38

Here Jesus gives us another antithesis (Mt. 5:1-12, See Page 64) to call attention to the plight of the less fortunate and the duty of his followers to tend to their needs:

> *At the sight of the crowds, his heart was moved with pity for them because they were troubled and abandoned, like sheep without a shepherd. Then he said to his disciples, "**The harvest is abundant but the laborers are few**; so ask the master of the harvest to send out laborers for his harvest."*

Jesus' words here echo a familiar theme seen throughout his ministry and call to his followers to tend to the welfare of orphans, needy children, the sick, and the poor. Today, Christianity remains in the forefront of groups whose works of charity and compassion extend to all those in need regardless of their beliefs. Happily, so it is with many other organizations and much of society in general. This was not so in the time of Jesus, and his words and actions continue to inspire many to sacrifice their time, wealth, and energy to work in third world nations.

The Mission of the Twelve Apostles

Matthew 10:1-40

Since Jesus charged his disciples to carry his message to the world following his death, it is relevant to enter what he said to them about their mission. Those instructions are summarized here. In Matthew 10, Jesus summoned his Twelve Apostles and instructed them to carry his words throughout Judea, proclaiming *"the kingdom of heaven is at hand"* (Matthew 10:7) and charging them to cure the sick, drive out demons and perform other acts, but to take no recompense. Jesus tells his disciples to take no earthly possessions with them, as they will find food and shelter when it is needed, and to leave any house or town where either is not offered, and to *"Shake the dust from your feet" (Matthew 10:14).*

In Matthew 10:15-25 Jesus warns his disciples they will be persecuted for their actions, and in Matthew 10:26-33 he tells his disciples not to be afraid, as man can kill the body but not the soul, and he assures them that God will know of their sacrifice, since *"even the hairs of your head are counted" (Matthew 10:30).*

In Matthew 10:34-36 Jesus tells his disciples that his mission will not bring peace to the Jews but instead will be the cause of much turmoil among them and set *a "man against his father, a daughter against her mother" (Matthew. 10:35)*, foreshadowing the rejection and persecution that will follow him and his disciples.

In Matthew 10:37-42 Jesus tells his disciples that they must love him above all and that *"whoever does not take up my cross* * *and follow after me is not worthy of me" (Matthew 10:38).*

Matthew 10 concludes as Jesus tells his disciples that the rewards his followers will receive will be great, and *"Whoever receives you receives me, and whoever receives me receives the one who sent me" (Matthew 10:40).*

---

* This is the first time that Jesus uses the term "take up the cross" in the Gospels. Jesus is clearly foreshadowing his crucifixion, which was a form of capital punishment used by the Romans for those who were not Roman citizens, such as slaves. *"Follow after me"* foreshadows the same fate is to be suffered by his Apostles.

John the Baptist is Arrested
Matthew 11:2-19

After Jesus charged his disciples to follow in his footsteps, he continued his public ministry and was greeted by followers of John the Baptist, who advise Jesus that John has been arrested. They tell Jesus that John has sent them to ask if he is truly the Messiah, the chosen one of God. Jesus, who was baptized by John, tells them to go and tell him of the many miracles they see and hear *"the blind regain their sight, the lame walk... and the poor have the good news proclaimed to them."* Jesus continues by praising John's virtues to the gathered crowd and completes the discourse with the words *"But wisdom is vindicated by her works."*

John the Baptist is venerated as a Saint by many Christian churches, and is considered a prophet in the Qur'an and a number of other faiths, as well. To non-Christians, John the Baptist may be the second most recognizable figure in the Gospels. Certainly, the portrayal of his beheading, discussed on Page 98, is one of the more dramatical biblical scenes that have found their way into modern culture. Of significance, he is the only figure (besides Jesus) identified by name in non-Christian writings dating from the first century.[71]

Jesus' Promise to His Followers
Matthew 11:28

Here Jesus promises his followers *"rest"* from their burdens if they follow his teachings. As with Jesus' use of parables to convey an underlying message, he was not speaking of relief from one's physical burdens here, but rather of spiritual and emotional release from sorrow, despair and worldly temptations, which would be replaced by peace of mind and inner happiness.

> ***"Come to me, all you who labor and are burdened, and I will give you rest.*** *Take my yoke upon you and learn from me, for I am meek and humble of heart; and you will find rest for yourselves. For my yoke is easy, and my burden light."*

It can be further postulated that the *"rest"* that Jesus has promised for taking up his *"yoke"* is that which frees one of the self. As with any similar spiritual following, its achievement is not without sacrifice and, on occasion, ostracism and even persecution – witness China's continuing oppression of the Buddhist monks and nuns of Tibet, and the crimes committed against Christians and Jews by religious extremists.

While some may view the loss of self in the pursuit of inner peace as self-delusional, the true loss of the self relates to the ability to let go of one's ego, which few of us are willing or capable of doing. While a healthy ego gives us our individuality, knowing when to surrender it, and the ability to do so, is just as important, but much more difficult. There is a saying among followers of Jesus that addresses this difficulty; when presented with an issue that challenges their ego, they can simply ask themselves "What would Jesus do?" As entered earlier, Jesus' teachings can provide us with a road map and unerring compass to help make that decision.

Jesus Breaks the Sabbath

Matthew 12:1-26

Matthew Chapter 12 describes Jesus' continued confrontations with the Jewish leaders of his time, because they believed his teachings and actions were heretical. In Matthew 12:1-8 Jesus is accused of breaking the Sabbath,[72] by the gathering of grain (so that he and his disciples might eat), and by ministering to the sick who are brought to him, both of which acts were considered a breach of the law. After Jesus drove out a demon from a man who had been brought to him on the Sabbath, the Pharisees claim that his power must come from Beelzebub (the devil). In reply, Jesus responds in words that continue to resonate, even to this very day:

> *"Every kingdom divided against itself will be laid waste, and no town or* ***house divided against itself will stand.*** *And if Satan drives out Satan, he is divided against himself; how, then, will his kingdom stand?" (Matthew 12:25)*

Abraham Lincoln used almost the exact words in his famous "House Divided" speech[73], given in Springfield, Illinois, at the State Capital in June of 1858. The speech foreshadowed the Civil War, which commenced three years later. Lincoln's words were clearly inspired by this passage and his view that the issue of slavery was dividing the country. This now famous speech can be found inscribed on the walls of the Lincoln Memorial in Washington, DC.

The Parable of the Sower

Matthew 13:1-53

Jesus' next great public discourse comes to us in Matthew 13. Here, Jesus speaks to a crowd who had come to hear him in Galilee, using seven parables to describe his ministry and heaven. The first of these parables is known as the *"Sower,"* who casts seeds on untilled ground (which was the custom of farmers, who would till after the seeds had been spread). In Matthew 13:18 Jesus explains to his disciples the meaning of the parable, likening himself to the sower and his words to the seeds. Those that fell on rich soil (those who hear his words and take them to heart) will yield an abundant crop, and those that fell on shallow ground will soon wither and die.

Other parables in Matthew 13 include *"weeds among wheat,"* which will be consumed by fire during the harvest; the parable of the *"mustard seed,"* which, although the smallest of seeds*, produces a very large tree; and *"yeast,"* which causes bread to rise many times.

Jesus' use of the parables is also a call to reflection for those who would be his followers. Like *"rich soil,"* only those who are prepared to seek a deeper meaning in these allegorical phrases can truly come to understand Jesus and gain a greater appreciation of his message. While some Christian traditionalists believe that the written word of the Gospels must be accepted verbatim, Jesus' use of parables asks us to seek a deeper meaning, by contemplation, as someone once said, "to see the truth as God gives us the light to see it."

Jesus is Rejected in His Hometown

Matthew 13:54-58

When Jesus had finished talking to the crowd he left Galilee and returned to his hometown of Nazareth, where he began to speak to the people in the synagogue. While Matthew notes that the people were amazed at what Jesus had to say, they also ques-

---

* The mustard seed is about the size of a small grape pit; a full-grown tree can reach a height and width of ten to fifteen feet or more. Jesus' parable of the "mustard seed" (Matthew 13:1-33) foreshadowed the growth of his following from the tiny nucleus of his early disciples to the vast following of today. Christianity comprises over one-third of the world's population. It would seem that those with "the faith of a mustard seed" can "move mountains" after all. (Matthew 17:20, See Page 104)

tioned how he spoke to them as if he were one of status, asking:

> *"Is he not the carpenter's son? Is not his mother named Mary and his brothers James, Joseph, Simon, and Judas? Are not his sisters all with us?"* And they took offense at him. But Jesus said to them,* ***"A prophet is not without honor except in his native place and in his own house."***†

This event is also entered in Luke 4:16 to 30, including the people's skepticism and Jesus' response to their apparent aversion to his apparent chastisement of them: *"Surely you will quote me this Proverb* ***'Physician, Cure Yourself?'****"*

Like the earlier Gospel passages which contain Jesus' admonishment of those who would judge others, the above proverb (the reader may by more familiar KJV "Physician Heal Thyself" – Luke 4:23) reminds us to attend to our own shortcomings rather than criticize those of others. The first proverb may also remind the reader of situations they experienced in their own life, perhaps when promoted over others in a workplace or in trying to overcome a nickname that stuck from childhood. As one of the Nazarenes asked his townsmen, *"Was not this Joseph's boy?"* The underlying message can still be seen today, such as in our armed forces which routinely transfer those promoted to positions of leadership to avoid their having to give orders to former buddies; large corporations sometimes do the same.

---

* As entered in Page 36, above, those who have cited this passage as proof that Jesus had brothers and sisters (a fact disputed by many Christian denominations), may have done so due to a misinterpretation of words translated from the Greek language in which the Gospels were written. However, the issue is moot as far as this writing is concerned, since its intent is only to illuminate Jesus' teachings.

† The reader may be more familiar with variations of this phrase, including "no prophet is accepted in his hometown."

John the Baptist is Beheaded
Matthew 14:3-13

One of the more dramatic stories to come down to us from the New Testament, which was recorded in antiquity, involves the arrest and execution of John the Baptist by order of the tetrarch of Galilee, Herod Antipas. Because John figured prominently in the ministry of Jesus, including what is entered at Page 139 below, some mention of his life and death is warranted. John is revered as a prophet by Christians, and had a great following, some of whom may have become Jesus' Apostles. John baptized sinners in the Jordan River and admonished them to righteousness toward each other and devoutness toward God.

In what has now become a famous reenactment, Matthew 14 describes the beheading of John the Baptist to fulfill a birthday promise Herod made to his stepdaughter Salome, whose dancing so delighted him that he offered her any gift she would ask, up to one-half of his kingdom. Prompted by her mother Herodias, Salome demanded John's head on a platter, in retribution for his having repeatedly called Herodias a harlot for divorcing the tetrarch's half-brother Phillip to marry Herod.

One of the phrases which have come down to us concerning John the Baptist, "***a voice of one crying out in the desert***" (Mark 1:3) or the more familiar "a voice crying out in the wilderness" (KJV) comes from John the Baptist's mission and has found its way into our culture, including as the title page of a book published by the Illinois State Historical Society and as the motto "*Vox clamantis in deserto*" (the voice of one crying out in the wilderness) of Dartmouth College in Hanover, New Hampshire, one of nine colonial colleges established before the American Revolution.

Jesus Performs a Miracle – Foreshadowing the Last Supper

Matthew 14:13-21

Matthew 14 continues with the recounting of miracles performed by Jesus. Only one will be discussed here, as it has a special meaning to all Christians, and has led to perhaps the most misunderstood of all Christian practices, the celebration of "The Last Supper" at Mass (Page 150, Matthew 26: 26-30), below. Matthew Chapter 14:13-21 describes many thousands being fed as five loaves of bread and two fish were multiplied.

What Defiles Man

Matthew 15:1-11

In Matthew 15:1-20 Jesus is again confronted by the Pharisees for breaking Jewish tradition by failing to require his disciples to wash their hands before eating. In response Jesus calls them hypocrites, citing scripture and, calling the attention of a crowd, says:

> *"It is not what enters one's mouth that defiles that person; but what comes out of the mouth is what defiles one."*

When asked to explain this by his disciples, Jesus tells them that whatever enters the body through the mouth passes through the body and is expelled but that which proceeds from the mouth comes from the heart and defiles. The contemporariness of this phrase could not be more compelling.

"The Blind Leading the Blind"

Matthew 15:12-14

Jesus uses another term that has come down to us as part of everyday usage. When told by his disciples that his words have angered the Pharisees he responds:

> *"Let them alone; they are blind guides [of the blind].* ***If a blind person leads a blind person, both will fall into a pit."***

The "blind leading the blind" is an oft-used metaphor today to describe situations where a lack of comprehension or awareness can lead to lead to calamity. Juan Mascaró's translation of the *Upanishads* may have captured it best: "Abiding in the midst of ignorance, thinking themselves wise and learned, fools go aimlessly hither and thither, like blind led by the blind."

8 Matthew Chapters 16 and 17

Introduction

The significance of Matthew 16 is that it is the first time Jesus foretells of his coming "Passion" and confers on Peter the power to carry forth his authority on earth. Several of Jesus' sayings in Matthew 16 that have come down to us in everyday use and are entered hereunder. Today, the word "passion" is used to describe an all-encompassing love of an object or person. This is remarkable when one considers the origin of the word.*

Jesus' ministry continues in Matthew 17 with an event that is seminal to the Apostles. It draws upon the Old Testament and non-canonical Jewish apocalyptic literature that describe God's presence in the form of a brilliant light, white garments, and an overshadowing cloud. Matthew 17 also includes the second time that Jesus foretells of his coming Passion to his disciples.

"The Sign of the Times"
Matthew 16:1-12

In Matthew 16:1-12 Jesus is again confronted by Church Elders

---

* The word "passion" comes from the Greek word *paschein*, which means "to suffer," and its use in the Gospels refers to the last week of Jesus' life, commencing with his "triumphal" entry into Jerusalem and includes the "Last Supper," the "Agony in the Garden," as well as Jesus' arrest, trial, crucifixion, and resurrection. Christians commemorate this period as "Holy Week," starting on Palm Sunday and ending on Easter Sunday.

and once more answers their charges using scripture. In the opening passage of the chapter, the Pharisees and the Sadducees demand that Jesus give them *"a sign from heaven"* that he is the Messiah. Jesus answers in words that appear as sarcasm when he responds with a very old adage we now recognize as a common sailor's saw, "red sky at night, sailors delight, red sky . . . " (In Jesus' time, the word "shepherd" was used in place of "sailor.") Jesus concludes his response to the Pharisees and Sadducees with the following words:

> *"You know how to judge the appearance of the sky, but you cannot judge* ***the signs of the times"*** *(Mt. 16:3).*

The term "sign of the times" has been frequently used to describe events that are less than complimentary, typically involving some less than acceptable behavior by some individual or group. The term has found its way into music as well as other media, and even served as the title to a number one recording by British singer Petula Clark in the 1960s, "A Sign of the Times."

The Keys to the Kingdom
Matthew 16:13-19

In Matthew 16:13-16 Jesus asks his disciples, *"Who do the people say is the Son of Man?"* Their answers indicate that they do not understand what Jesus is asking, so he then says, *"But who do you say that I am?"* Peter, who was the first Apostle called, answers, *"You are the Messiah, the Son of the living God."* Jesus says in reply:

> *"And so I say to you,* ***you are Peter, and upon this rock I will build my church****, and the gates of the netherworld shall not prevail against it. I will give you* ***the keys to the kingdom*** *of heaven. Whatever you bind on earth shall be bound in heaven; and whatever you loose*

on earth shall be loosed in heaven" (Mt. 16:18-19).

Today, Roman Catholics recognize Peter as the first pope. Since Rome was his home until his martyrdom, his direct followers were viewed as the successive keepers of the keys and the great basilica was built where he was believed to have been crucified. Tradition holds that Peter was crucified upside down as he believed he was not worthy to die as Jesus had.* Today Saint Peter's is the seat of the Roman Catholic Church, known as Vatican City, and is considered an independent country by Italy.

The Conditions of Discipleship
Matthew 16:24-26

Jesus tells a gathered crowd that they must deny themselves by taking up his cross and following him, if they wish to be saved. His words on that occasion are both poetic and deeply meaningful.

> ***"What profit is there for one to gain the whole world and forfeit his life?"†***

Jesus uses the word "life" to mean the eternal soul. Many similar passages can be found throughout the Gospels, and the precept of the denial of material things for moral imperatives can be found throughout the world's religions and ascetic philosophies. At its heart is the principle that calls us to disown ourselves as the center of our existence. Its practice, while

---

* Shortly before Jesus was arrested, Peter said he would never abandon him. Jesus replied *"Amen, I say to you, this very night before the cock crows, you will deny me three times." (Matthew 26:34)*

† The King James Version of the passage may be more familiar to the reader "For what shall it profit a man, if he shall gain the whole world, and lose his own soul?"

seemingly impractical in today's world, can be facilitated by acts of charity, empathy, and love. Parallels to Jesus' words can be found in a few expressions that may be familiar to the reader, such as "you can't take it with you" and "What we do for ourselves dies with us. What we do for others and the world remains and is immortal." (Albert Pike)

Jesus' Transfiguration

Matthew 17:1-8

Matthew tells of Jesus going to the top of a mountain, accompanied by three of his disciples. When they reach the top Jesus is transformed; his face *"shines like the sun and his clothes become white as light."*

Moses and the prophet Elijah then appear and converse with Jesus. As they are talking, a bright cloud overshadows them and a voice coming from the cloud says, *"This is my beloved Son, with whom I am well pleased; listen to him."* At this the disciples prostrate themselves. When they look up, only Jesus remains.

The reader may question the entry of this passage, since it is not Jesus' words that are recorded, however, this is the only time the Gospels report of any Apostle hearing the word of God. It is only included as background to what is to follow Jesus' death, and the amazing sacrifices his disciples made to carry on his legacy.

Jesus Tells His Disciples to Have Faith

Matthew 17:20

After Jesus returned from the mountain he is greeted by a crowd and is asked to cure a young boy who is possessed. The father asks Jesus to heal the boy, as the disciples were unable to do so.

Jesus removes the demons that had plagued the boy and chastises his disciples, telling them they were unable to heal the boy because their faith was too weak.

> *"He said to them, 'Because of your little faith. Amen, I say to you,* ***if you have faith the size of a mustard seed,*** *you will say to this mountain, move from here to there, and it will move.* ***Nothing will be impossible for you.'"***

Jesus uses the parable of the faith the size of a mustard seed more than once, including in Matthew 13:31. The seed of the mustard plant is not much larger than the head of a pin, yet the full-grown plant can exceed a height of fifteen feet! Interestingly, there exist Jewish theological works that compare the size of the universe to a mustard seed, to show the insignificance of our world and to teach humility. The Jewish philosopher Nahmanides wrote that the universe expanded from the time of its creation, at which point it was the size of a mustard seed.[74] (Shades of the Big Bang Theory?)

9 Matthew Chapters 18 to 20

Introduction

Matthew Chapters 18 to 20 encompass the last accounts of Jesus' public ministry which precede his entry into Jerusalem, where he will be tried and condemned to death. Following this, selected passages taken from the Gospels of Mark, Luke, and John, which also preceded Jesus' entry into Jerusalem, will be entered. In Matthew 18, Jesus begins to teach his disciples how they are to carry on after he is gone. He uses parables to instruct them in humility, temptation, redemption, the exercise of authority, and forgiveness. Jesus' parables contain truths that are worthy of contemplation.

The Greatest in the Kingdom

Matthew 18:1-5

When asked by his disciples who would be found to be the greatest in heaven, Jesus calls a child to him and responds:

> *"Whoever humbles himself like this child is the greatest in the kingdom of heaven. And whoever receives one child such as this in my name receives me."*

Christian theology explains that Jesus' parable is a metaphor calling his disciples to true humility, such as that of a child's total dependence and trust toward his or her parents. It also reminds us that whatever we do for those who may be the least visible to society will be seen as great in the eyes of the more discerning.

Those Who Lead a Child Astray

Matthew 18:6-9

In Matthew 18:1-5 above, Jesus calls upon his disciples to be as accepting of his father's will as a child is of its parents. Here Jesus warns his disciples to protect these "little ones" against sin, damning those who do not and exclaiming:

> *"Whoever causes one of these little ones . . . to sin, it would be better for him to have a great millstone hung around his neck and to be drowned in the depths of the sea."*

Jesus' words here echo what most consider one of modern society's greatest responsibilities; the protection and fostering of children. This was not so in Jesus' time, or any time up to the recent past, for that matter. Indeed, children's rights are a relatively modern concern, with the first laws protecting them only coming about in response to their abuse during the Industrial Revolution. (see also Matthew 19:13-15 at Page 110 as entered below.)

The Parable of the Lost Sheep Who is Found

Matthew 18:10-14

Jesus' parable of *"The lost sheep,"* which when found brought more joy to the shepherd than the ninety-nine that did not stray, is obviously a metaphor for a sinner. The symbolism of a sheep wandering from the fold is a recurrent theme in the Gospels and is analogous to the parable of the prodigal son. Since Luke 15:1-7 (See Page 126) includes the verse familiar to most Christians, it will be discussed thereunder.

Judgment of Transgressors – Trial by One's Peers
Matthew 18:15-20

Here Jesus tells his disciples what they must do if one of the members transgresses. The first step requires a disciple to meet the offender in private. If the wrongdoer does not repent, then two or three of the members are to meet the offender. If still unrepentant, the offender is to be brought before the entire community. If the offender does not repent, then he or she is to be expelled. Jesus gives his disciples the authority to do this in a verse that is familiar to all Christians and possibly to many others:

> *"For where two or three are gathered together in my name, there am I in the midst of them."*

While trials were not new to Jesus' time, they were presided over by people of higher rank, whereas Jesus instructs his disciples to convene a group of the transgressor's peers, foreshadowing our modern court proceedings.

Forgiveness and the Unmerciful Servant
Matthew 18:21-35

Jesus' final discourse in Matthew 18 answers a question posed by the Apostle Peter regarding how many times a transgression should be forgiven. When Peter suggests seven times, Jesus answers,

> *"Not seven times but seventy-seven times."*

To emphasize the point, Jesus then tells his disciples a parable of a servant whose debt is forgiven by a merciful master, while the servant later refuses to forgive the debt owed to him by another. Upon learning of this, the master demands the repayment of the servant's previously forgiven debt and turns him over to torturers until the debt is repaid in full.

Jesus' parable tells us that we must forgive others if we expect others to forgive us. A 12-step publication contains a remarkable passage about forgiveness. It states that the only true road to forgiveness is to set aside one's ego. If we do that, then there are no insults or perceived injustices, as the only thing that would be injured is something that no longer controls our emotions, such as pride.

Introduction to Matthew Chapters 19 and 20

Matthew Chapters 19 and 20 mark the last of Jesus' public ministry before entering his Passion. Chapter 19 commences as Jesus leaves Galilee to make a pilgrimage to the Great Temple in Jerusalem in preparation for Passover,[75] as was the custom. Jesus meets large crowds and Pharisees along the way. The narrative that follows attempts to capture some of what transpired.

Marriage and Divorce

Matthew 19:1-12

Jesus' Sermon on the Mount, and particularly his denunciation of those who divorce their wives, (Matthew 5:31, See Page 69) reached the ears of the Pharisees, who went to confront him as he was speaking to a great crowd who were following him at that time. They asked Jesus if were lawful for a man to divorce his wife.[76] Jesus responds by explaining that it is not legal for a man to divorce his wife, as God had ordained that they be joined together as one flesh (Gn. 2:24).

Jesus concludes with words that will be familiar to anyone who has attended a formal Christian marriage:

> *"Therefore, what God has joined together, no human being must separate."* *

Realizing the strictness of these words, his disciples asked Jesus if it were better not to marry at all. While the Gospels include many passages which affirm Jesus' positive view of marriage, he agrees that adherence to his teaching on divorce[77] will be difficult, but says only those who cannot fulfill the requirements for marriage should remain celibate:

> *"Some are incapable of marriage because they were born so; some, because they were made so by others; some, because they have renounced marriage, for the sake of the kingdom of heaven. Whoever can accept this ought to accept it."*

Jesus Blesses the Children

Matthew 19:13-15

Matthew continues in 19 with a recurrent theme in Jesus' ministry, his love of children. Here, numbers of the crowd attempt to bring their children to Jesus for a blessing, but his disciples, sensing Jesus is tired, resist this. Jesus, seeing this, tells his disciples:

> *"Let the children come to me, and do not prevent them; for the kingdom of heaven belongs to such as these."*

Here again Jesus tells his disciples the importance of cherishing children, whose innocence is incomparable.† Given Jesus' repeated admonishments regarding the care and treatment of

---

* The KJV contains perhaps the more common "What God has joined together, let not man put asunder."

† My mother had a unique way of expressing this; "When you kiss a baby (or child), you touch heaven." See also Matthew 18:1-5 and Matthew 18:6-9, Pages 106-107)

children, the sexual abuse of children by members of the clergy is tragic, heartbreaking, and frankly astounding. The Roman Catholic Church, which is by far the largest of all Christian denominations, is seen by many (and rightfully so) as having committed the most egregious crimes. However, while garnering the most publicity, Catholic clergy are not alone in the commission of these terrible atrocities; studies have regrettably shown that the incidence of reported cases of child abuse among other religious groups and Christian denominations is as common, and no less distressing. Thankfully, the Roman Catholic Church has finally taken extraordinary steps to prevent such abuses from ever happening again.

The Rich Young Man

Matthew 19:16-24

While Jesus is preaching to the crowd, a rich young man comes forward and asks what he must do to gain eternal life. Jesus tells the young man that he must sell his possessions and give the proceeds to the poor;[78] he will then be ready to follow Jesus, as one of his disciples. Matthew writes that the young man went away sad, as he had many possessions. Jesus, senses this, and tells his disciples:

> *"Again I say to you, it is easier for a camel to pass through the eye of a needle than for one who is rich to enter the kingdom of God."*

Upon reflection, the reader may conclude that nothing has changed much since Jesus walked the earth. The greedy and power-seekers still abound and continue to multiply. In fact, the *"narrow gate"* to salvation that Jesus talked about in Matthew 7:13-14 above (See Page 84) has seemingly become narrower.

Those Who Will Be Saved

Matthew 19:25-30

When they hear Jesus' words of how difficult it is for someone with possessions to enter heaven his disciples ask,

> *"Who then can be saved?" (Matthew 19:25).*

Jesus replies that those who faithfully follow him will have eternal life and gives them a phrase whose theme is also recurrent in his teachings:

> *"But many who are first will be last, and the last will be first."*

Jesus uses this expression repeatedly throughout his ministry, and particularly in the passage that follows directly below. While society needs leaders in every field of human endeavor, Jesus admonished his disciples to lead by their example of service to others. Indeed, many who find success in their lives feel compelled to use their position and wealth to give back to society some of what they have earned.

The Parable of the Vineyard Workers

Matthew 20:1-16

In one of the more memorable and vivid passages Jesus tells his disciples a parable about a landowner of a vineyard who hires workers early one morning for the "usual wage," which was a denarius at that time. Later, he finds others waiting to be hired and sends them to the same vineyard. Toward mid-afternoon, he again finds other workers and sends them to the vineyard. In the evening the landowner tells his foremen to bring the workers to him for their pay, starting with the ones hired last, and in turn, pays all the workers a full day's wages. At this, the workers who had been hired early in the day began to grumble, complaining:

> *"These last ones worked only one hour, and you have made them equal to us, who bore the day's burden and the heat. He said to one of them in reply, 'My friend, I am not cheating you. Did you not agree with me for the usual daily wage? Take what is yours and go. What if I wish to give this last one the same as you? Am I not free to do as I wish with my own money? Are you envious because I am generous? Thus,* ***the last will be first, and the first will be last.****'"*

The purpose of Jesus' parable here is not difficult to grasp. While the parable seems foolish on the surface, Jesus is obviously telling his disciples, and all of us, that it is never too late to change our lives for the better, and those who do should be granted pardon. However, since no one knows the day or hour when they will take their last breath, Christians see those who put off "repenting" as gambling with their eternal souls (See Luke 12:13-34, Page 121).

The Son of Man Came to Serve
Matthew 20:20-28

Matthew Chapter 20 concludes as Jesus tells his disciples of the coming "Passion" (See footnote, Page 101). Upon hearing this, the mother of two of the disciples asks Jesus to give her sons a place of honor at his side when he comes into his heavenly kingdom. At this, the other disciples become indignant and an argument ensues as to who most deserving of the honor. Hearing this, Jesus replies:

> ***"Whoever wishes to be great among you shall be your servant;*** *whoever wishes to be first among you shall be your slave. Just so, the Son of Man did not come to be served but to serve and to give his life as a ransom for many."*

Jesus' words here have special meaning to all Christians, as the foundation of Christianity rests on the belief that Jesus sacrificed himself for the forgiveness of mankind's sins. We have all heard the saying that there is no greater sacrifice than one who lays down his life for a friend. Christians believe that Jesus' selfless act of surrender to be tortured and nailed to a cross was a symbol of his great love for all humanity and that it is a wondrous thing to be so loved.

The final Chapters in Matthew (21 to 28) record the last week of his Jesus' life and the events that followed his crucifixion. Passages from these last chapters of Matthew will be entered after those taken from the Gospels of Mark, Luke and John, which now follow. Selected passages from these three Gospels are entered as their phrasing may be more familiar to the reader, and/or because they were not recorded in Matthew's Gospel.

10 The Gospel According to Mark

Introduction

Mark's Gospel was written in Greek and probably for a gentile audience, based on Mark's need to explain Jewish traditions and translate Aramaic terms. The most currently accepted view is that Mark was completed before 70 AD which was the year that the Great Temple was destroyed in Jerusalem by the Romans. Jesus had predicted this event would occur within the lifetime of the Apostles. Historians have reasoned that had Mark been written after such a major event, it would have been given more prominence in the Gospel to support Jesus' message, and the Apostles' mission. This was also discussed in section 1, above (Historicity of the Gospels).

Mark was not one of Jesus' 12 Apostles and is believed to have been the Apostle Peter's translator in Rome, where Peter was crucified. Since Mark is the shortest of all four Gospels at 16 Chapters, and lacks the detail provided in Matthew (which spans 28 Chapters), much of Jesus' teachings reported in this book were taken from the latter. For this reason, only Mark 8:14-21 follows. Other entries from Mark include Mark 16:15-16 "Did Jesus Condemn Non-Christians?" (Page 38), Jesus Talks About Divorce (Mark 14:3-7. Mark 10:12), and "The Anointing in Bethany" (Page 137).

The "Leaven" of the Pharisees

Mark 8:14-21

Jesus devoted a good part of his ministry to teaching his Apostles, which at times proved frustrating to him, as they did not always grasp his meaning. One such time occurred when Jesus used the word "leavening" as a metaphor to explain to his followers that just as bread dough increases dramatically when leavened with yeast, so would the populace's opposition to his ministry grow, due to the corruptive authority of the Pharisees. He also tells his disciples that in the same vein his words are like yeast, as they will yield many converts. When he realizes his disciples do not grasp his meaning, Jesus chastises them, saying:

"Do you have eyes and not see, ears and not hear?"

As on many prior occasions, Jesus drew on his knowledge of scripture to make a point. These words appear to have been taken directly from the Old Testament, Ez.12:1-2. In this passage, God's chosen are cautioned about their rebellious nature. Jesus' warning here is relevant today, given the reports of widespread social and moral apathy and the ability of a charismatic leader to sway the judgment of many. The history of man is written in the blood and misery of many who blindly followed one despot or another.

While Jesus' words were uttered as a warning about the power of Herod and the Church Elders of his day, the phrase can also signify man's apathy to the plight of the poor, as employed to dramatic effect in a scene in the 1951 movie *A Christmas Carol.* The scene takes place as Ebenezer Scrooge (played by Alistair Sim) goes to his long-estranged nephew's house to accept a previously spurned dinner invitation. When he arrives, to the amazement of all present, Scrooge takes the hand of his nephew Fred's wife and says, "Can you forgive a pig-headed old fool for having no eyes to see with and no ears to hear with all these years."* Dickens' work was both an account of his own condition, and an indictment of his countrymen that they might open their eyes and ears to the deplorable conditions under which the lower classes lived. Indeed, the life expectancy of the poor in London at that time was not more than twenty-two years. Cavemen had a longer life expectancy! Perhaps the worst blindness is not the loss of sight.

---

* This wording doesn't appear to be in the original text of the book; it is likely that they were written into the movie script to emphasize Scrooge's transformation, and the timelessness of man's continued blindness to the needs of the poor.

11 The Gospel According to Luke

Introduction

Luke was the only non-Jew to have written a Gospel. Early Christian writings tell us that Luke (the name is a contraction of Lucilius) was a Syrian/Greek physician who lived in Antioch in ancient Syria. Today, Luke is venerated as a saint by the Roman Catholic Church and is believed to have died a martyr. Since Luke's Gospel also parallels Matthew's, only selected passages will be entered here.

In addition to the following passages, others were recorded earlier, including "The Prodigal Son" (Luke 15:11-32, Page 54), "The Parable of the Persistent Widow" (Luke. 18:1-7, Page 43), and "The Widow's Offering" (Luke 21:1-4, Page 44)

The Parable of the Lamp

Luke 8:16-18

In Luke Chapter 8 Jesus again instructs his disciples using parables, most of which were described in passages entered in Matthew, above. Luke employed two phrases in his Gospel that have come down to us in common usage, they occur as Jesus tells his disciples that their faith is like a lamp which will illuminate his message, so that others may ***"see the light,"*** and that what is not seen or known will ***"come to light."***

These phrases have come down to us in literature, music, and daily speech. The interesting thing here for us to consider is

Jesus' repeated use of the word "light" as a metaphor for himself and his teachings. Today the word is synonymous for becoming aware of something or of knowledge or understanding – figuratively, "I see the light."

"The Good Samaritan"
Luke 10:29-37

Here, Jesus again instructs his disciples using a parable that has become synonymous with someone who helps a stranger. The parable is about a wayfarer who is set upon by robbers, severely beaten, and left to die in a ditch alongside a well-traveled road.[79] Many who pass cross the road to avoid him, but a Samaritan[80] who is moved to compassion, stops and binds the man's wounds. The Samaritan then brings the injured man to an inn and gives the innkeeper money sufficient to provide for the man's recovery. In choosing to use a Samaritan, Jesus is clearly telling his disciples that they are to minister to *all* men, even if doing so risked the scorn of those who they sought to influence.

This parable has gained such widespread appeal that many states have enacted legislation known as "Good Samaritan Laws," to prevent lawsuits from being instituted against those who render well intentioned assistance to injured persons, which might later be judged as injurious. However, on the other side of the coin, we have all heard of stories of someone who is hurt or even being assaulted as others pass by, or even look on without offering assistance; many of us have even seen videos being taken of heinous acts, as if the importance lay in the spectacle, rather than in rendering assistance. Unfortunately, apathy and the unwillingness to help others has been one of the main sources of power for tyrants and oppressors of freedom throughout history.

The reader may also find the parable reminiscent of the saying "Am I my brother's keeper?" which is taken from the Old Testament story of Cain and Abel (Gn. 4:9). In the biblical account Cain murdered his brother Abel out of jealousy. God knows this and asks Cain where his brother is; Cain answers, "I do not know. Am I my brother's keeper?" In punishment, Cain is exiled to the land of "Nod," which is not a place but a word meaning "to wander." Cain's words have come to embody an unwillingness to help others, in contrast to the story of the good Samaritan. The moral here also poses the question, if I am not my brother's keeper, then who will be mine, in times of need?

Courage Under Persecution
Luke 12:2-9

Luke Chapter 12 is rich in phrases that have come down to us from Jesus' teachings, some of which are summarized hereunder. In 12:2-9 Luke includes several passages where Jesus inspires his followers to carry forth his message fearlessly, since those who would persecute them can only kill the body. He assures the Apostles that God is watching over them constantly, saying:

> *"Even the hairs of your head have all been counted"*
> *(Luke 12:7)*

Jesus' words also remind us here that no good deed goes unnoticed, if not by humankind then by the person who is helped. As important, it will become a receipt-less deposit into the account of self-worth. Moreover, good deeds are highly contagious; how many times have we heard someone say that they were inspired by a stranger's act of kindness to pass the gesture along to someone else in need or distress?

On Worldly Possessions

Luke 12:13-34

Luke 12:10-34 includes Jesus' words to those who would dedicate their lives to the gathering of material possessions, contrasting it with those who are confident that God will provide for their welfare. The disciples' detachment from material possessions would symbolize their belief that they are saving up treasure in heaven. In Luke 12:15 a man came out of the crowd and asked Jesus to give him justice by forcing his brother to share his wealth with him, to which Jesus replied:

> *"Take care to guard against all greed, for though one may be rich, one's life does not consist of possessions."*

Jesus continued in this vein with a parable of a rich man whose fields have yielded so abundantly that he plans to tear down his storage buildings so that he may build still larger ones, to increase his wealth. Congratulating himself for his forethought he thinks:

> *"Now as for you, you have so many good things stored up for many years, rest,* ***eat, drink, be merry!****" (Luke 12:19)*

Jesus tells the crowd the rich man should have been concerned with more than just increasing his wealth, as he will die before he can realize the gain his efforts will bring, saying:

> *"You fool, this night your life will be demanded of you; and the things you have prepared, to whom will they belong?" (Lk. 12:20)*

Jesus' words here are timeless; the relentless pursuit of wealth at the expense of all else is one of man's great follies. Gandhi expressed this as "commerce without morality" as part of what he labeled the "seven social sins."[81]

Luke contrasts the folly of the rich seeking worldly treasure with assurances that God will provide for his disciples every need and that they should not be apprehensive, adding:

> *"**Can any of you by worrying add a moment to your lifespan?** If even the smallest things are beyond your control, why are you anxious about the rest?" (Luke 12:25-26).*

Luke concludes these passages with Jesus again telling his disciples that they need not worry about material things but to rely on God to provide for their every need – and doing so will insure that they have stored up treasure that cannot be taken away or destroyed, saying:

> *"For where your treasure is, there also will your heart be" (Luke 12:34).*

It may be of some interest to the reader to know that the above verse was used by J. K. Rowling in the Harry Potter series, as a quotation carved on the family tomb of the headmaster of the school for wizards, Professor Albus Percival Wulfric Brian Dumbledore. That quotation reads: *"Where your treasure is, your heart will be also."*[82] Rowling used another biblical passage (1 Cor. 15:26) on the tombstone of Harry Potter's parents, which reads: ***"And the last enemy that shall be destroyed is death."***[83] (See "Jesus Explains the Resurrection" Matthew 22:23-33, Page 142.) While Ms. Rowling has not formally credited Christianity as having any influence on her writing, she did reportedly acknowledge the following during an Open Book Conference in 2007, where she was quoted as saying, "So on a very practical note, Harry was going to find biblical quotations on tombstones, [however] I think those two particular quotations he finds on the tombstones at Godric's Hollow . . . almost epitomize the whole series."

The Parable of the Faithful Servant
Luke 12:35-48

In Luke 12:42-48 Jesus uses a parable about a servant who is faithful to his master when charged with attending to his household while the master is away. When the master returns, he finds the servant has done well and rewards him accordingly. Jesus contrasts this with another servant who believing his master will be long in returning takes advantage of his position at the expense of the other servants and his master's food and wine.

When his master returns, the unfaithful servant is severely beaten and placed with the unfaithful (basically cast into hell). Jesus also tells his disciples that if the servant was not aware of the master's orders, he would not have been as severely punished.[84] Jesus concludes this parable with the following phrase, which has seen much use in modern times, albeit not in the same words:

> *"Much will be required of the person entrusted with much, and still more with the person to whom even more is entrusted" (Luke 12:48).*

Some may have heard the above expressed another way; with privilege comes responsibility, with responsibility comes accountability. We expect our elected officials to do what is best for the people who elect them, rather than what they see as the surest route to their reelection; we believe great athletes should be role models; we expect those with wealth to give proportionately to charity; and we expect those gifted with great intellect or talent to use these gifts to elevate mankind. Indeed, many so graced heed that call. How many times have we heard those so fortunate say they are only giving back to society?

We also see this when society comes to the aid of strangers who are stricken by a natural or man-made calamity. This phenomenon is unique to mankind. Certainly, it is rare to find another species that promotes the nurturing of its weakest members, or comes to the aid of outsiders. Where does this "humanity" come from, since it seems to run counter to the natural order of life, and the "survival of the fittest?" Many think this instinct comes from obedience to something greater than any of us, whether we choose to ascribe it to society, a higher power, or God.

The Parable of Invited Guests and Host
Luke 14:7-14

Jesus again uses a parable to instruct his disciples in humility and charity. Most readers have seen paintings and mosaics depicting how people were seated at a table when eating during the time of Jesus; Leonardo da Vinci's *Last Supper* is certainly the world's most famous painting (it's actually a fresco) of the setting. But Da Vinci used artistic license to show the faces of all the Apostles, as they are shown sitting or standing on either side of Jesus, whereas in reality chairs were not used at that time – the Apostles would have likely reclined at a rectangular table with Jesus at its head, as was customary for the host. In those days, guests of station would to be seated closest to the host, with people of lower rank seated further down the table. The tradition of seating guests by order of rank has not changed much since that time.

Jesus' parable is about a guest who takes a seat of honor, only to have his position taken by a late arriving guest who was of a higher rank. Since all the other places were presumably taken by then, the seated guest was forced into the embarrassing position of having to move to a place below his station. Jesus tells his disciples that when someone is invited to a banquet they should take a lower place at the table so that when the host comes he may say:

> *"My friend, move to a higher position. Then you will enjoy the esteem of your companions at the table."*

Jesus adds a phrase much repeated in the Gospels:

> *"For everyone who exalts himself will be humbled, but one who humbles himself will be exalted" (Luke 14:11).*

An example of Jesus' teachings being lived out today can be found in the life and career of Mariano Rivera, a man acknowledged throughout baseball as the greatest "closer" in the history of the sport, and holder of many relief-pitching records. While primarily known for an un-hittable "cutter," a pitch that broke so sharply into batters' hands that many were left holding the handle of a splintered bat, he was also universally known and admired for his grace in both victory and defeat, and the humility he expressed in refusing to take any credit for his phenomenal talent or coolness under fire, if you will.

While the strain of being a closer can be seen in the shortness of the careers of many closers, Rivera performed at a high level for over 19 years and closed out over 950 games, being credited with 652 "saves." When he announced his retirement, he was accorded an extraordinary outpouring of love and respect by opposing teams' players and fans alike, as he made his final visits to their home stadiums in 2013. Given that his team, the Yankees, are arguably the team many baseball fans love to hate, the accolades given him were remarkable and unprecedented.

Mariano's journey from an impoverished Panamanian fishing village to the top of the world of sports is an amazing story, one that punctuates Jesus' parable and personifies the meaning of the word humility. C. S. Lewis may have captured the essence of Jesus' parable best when he said "Humility is not thinking less of yourself, it's thinking of yourself less."

Jesus continued this dialogue, telling his disciples that if they host a celebration, rather than inviting friends and family, they should *"invite the poor, the crippled, the lame and the blind" (Luke 14:12-14)* as inviting the former cancels the gesture, since they may repay the host, whereas inviting the poor and infirm conveys true generosity, since they have no means of repayment.

Jesus' words to his disciples have perhaps more meaning today than they did when he uttered them two thousand years ago. In today's dog-eat-dog world we continually see ulterior motive masked as generosity. Our electoral process seems to be based more on political payback than service to a politician's constituency. While Jesus' words seem impossibly naïve in today's world, their truth is undeniable.

The Parable of the Lost Sheep

Luke 15:1-7

Luke 15 gives us three parables dealing with the redemption of sinners, the first being the parable of the lost sheep. The second parable, that of the lost coin, is followed by the parable of The Prodigal Son, which was included in the opening pages of this book (Page 54). Jesus used these parables to respond to criticisms levied against him by Pharisees and Scribes for allowing tax collectors and sinners to gather as he was speaking.* Jesus answered their accusations with the following parable:

> *"What man among you having a hundred sheep and losing one of them would not leave the ninety-nine in the desert and go after the lost one until he finds it? And when he does find it, he sets it on his shoulders with great joy and, upon his arrival home, he calls together his friends and neighbors and says to them, 'Rejoice with me because I have found my lost sheep.'* ***I tell you, in just the same way there will be more joy in heaven over one sinner who repents than over ninety-nine righteous people who have no need of repentance."***

The imagery of the lost sheep and Jesus depicting himself as the "Good Shepherd" (John 10:1-21, See Page 132) can be found throughout the Gospels. Parallels can be found in the Old Testament, including in the beloved Twenty-Third Psalm ("The Lord is my Shepherd") and Ezekiel 34 ("The Parable of the Shepherds"). The symbolism of the sheep and their shepherd is understandable, given the culture of the people of the Old Testament and Gospels. Many "pastors" (form the Latin word *pastorem* "Shepherd") continue to refer to their congregation as their "flock." While the word "sheep" is now used as a derogatory term to refer to people who blindly follow a leader or movement, Jesus used the term to instruct his followers to be gentle and observant of God's will, as sheep were to their shepherd.

---

* The reader will recall that one of Jesus' apostles, Matthew, was a tax collector.

12 The Gospel According to John

Introduction

The Gospel of John is quite different from the other Gospels in style and appears to have been written more for purposes of ministry than as a chronological account of Jesus' life and teachings. Catholic theologians also believe it was written by more than one person, and resolved into its present form between AD 90 and 100. [85] Since the most familiar of Jesus' teachings that have come down to us have been addressed earlier in this narrative, only a few of those contained within John's Gospel are entered here. In addition to the following, other memorable passages from John were entered above in section 1 "Jesus and the Woman of Samaria" (John 4:1-42), also in the book's Preface and at Page 50 (John 8:7).

Who May Enter the Kingdom of Heaven

John 3:1-21

This passage was initially discussed at Page 38, above. It is entered in its entirety here, because of its significance to so many Christians. As noted in the opening section of the book, many of the readers may have heard the term "born again" and perhaps the fact that various Christian denominations believe that Jesus condemned all those who do not accept his divinity. The term "born again" is as it's written in John 3 of the King James version (KJV). The term *"born from above"* is taken the Roman

Catholic Gospel of John and occurs when Jesus tells the Jewish Pharisee Nicodemus[86] what he must do to enter heaven:

> *"Amen, amen, I say to you, no one can see the kingdom of God without being born from above" (John 3:5)*

The passage continues:

> *For God did not send his Son into the world to condemn the world, but that the world might be saved through him. (John 3:17)*

John concludes:

> *Whoever believes in him will not be condemned, but whoever does not believe has already been condemned, because he has not believed in the name of the only Son of God. (John 3:18)* *

As recorded earlier, Roman Catholics do not believe that Jesus condemned those who did not believe in his divinity.

The Bread of Life

John 6:22-59

In Matthew 14:13-21 (See Page 99.), we are told that Jesus fed a crowd of thousands.† John's Gospel relates that when the crowd went to find him the next day, Jesus tells them that they only returned to be fed, rather than to hear his words. He admonishes them, saying:

> *"Do not work for food that perishes but food that*

---

* Catholic theologians have concluded that this was meant as a warning to Pharisees who had condemned Jesus for his teachings.

† While the intent of this narrative is only for readers to consider the wisdom of Jesus' teachings, it is necessary to provide the reader some detail of a few of the miracles described in the Gospels for context. The miracle here is the feeding of a large crowd, numbering in the thousands, from five barley loaves of bread and two fish.

endures for eternal life" (John 6:27).

When the crowd hears this, they ask Jesus what they might do to obtain this food; he tells them to believe in the one sent by God. The crowd asks for a sign that they may know that Jesus was sent by God, saying:

> *"Our ancestors ate manna [87] in the desert as it is written 'He gave them bread from heaven to eat'" (John 6:31).*

Jesus answers that it was not Moses who gave them bread but their Father in heaven:

> *My Father gives you the true bread from heaven" (John 6:32).*

The crowd then asks that they too may receive this bread; Jesus replies in words that foreshadow those he used at the time of the Last Supper,[88] which was to become the central part of Christian's daily religious services:

> ***"I am the bread of life,** whoever comes to me will never hunger and whoever believes in me will never thirst" (John 6:35).*

The Slavery of Sin

John 8:31-35

Here Jesus tells us that anyone who commits a sin is a "slave" and that comprehending this truth will set one free from the bondage of self-gratification. Jesus tells his followers that this "truth" will become self-evident in words that have come into common use:

> ***"You will know the truth, and the truth will set you free."***

Jesus' words here may be familiar to the reader; their Latin translation, *veritas liberabit vos* (literally, "the truth shall set you free"), has been used as a motto for uncounted schools and universities throughout the world and is inscribed prominently in the main lobby of the CIA headquarters at Langley, Virginia.

Today the truth seems hard to come by, with political correctness, ideological frames of reference, and *spinmeisters* who are paid to translate the English language for us. What more fitting words can one find than those uttered by Jesus in Matthew 5:33-37 (See Page 70).

> *"Let your 'Yes' mean 'Yes,' and your 'No' mean 'No.' Anything more is from the evil one."*

Jesus' call for us to be free of the slavery of compulsive behavior and selfishness is the foundation of many of the world's religious and ascetic philosophies. Their common denominator is the calling for their adherents to practice discipline and restraint regarding physical pleasure, personal conduct, and the pursuit of material things. These practices are not as much a rejection of the pleasures of life as they are means to physical and mental well-being and spiritual enlightenment.

The Man Born Blind - Jesus is the Light of the World
John 9:1-5

John Chapter 9 records Jesus' healing of a man blind from birth. Afterward, foreshadowing his death, Jesus tells his disciples that he must do the work of his Father *"while it is day [since] night is coming."* Jesus continues, uttering words that have great meaning for Christians:

> *"While I am in the world, I am the light of the world."*

Jesus uses the term "light" as a metaphor for himself and his teachings. Today we often use the word "light" as a symbol of knowledge and understanding. Interestingly, much of what we know about the universe comes to us in the form of light.

Jesus is the Good Shepherd
John 10:1-21

In John Chapter 10 Jesus continues clashing with the Pharisees, using the metaphor of a good shepherd. In these passages, Jesus tells the Pharisees that his followers know his voice and follow him, but will not follow the voice of a stranger.

> *"**I am the good shepherd.** A good shepherd lays down his life for the sheep . . . and I know mine and mine know me" (John 10:14).*

Jesus' use of this metaphor is given more meaning if the reader is acquainted with the fact that sheep recognize the voice of their shepherd and will follow him, and no other. Jesus' message was also intended as a warning that there would be many false prophets, whose nature would be known by the fruit they bore. The fruits Jesus bore were examples of love, forgiveness, charity, empathy, and the shunning of the pursuit of wealth or position for its own sake.

The Vine and the Branches
John 15:1-13

In John Chapter 15 Jesus tells his disciples that he is the vine and they are the branches, and just as the branches cannot bear fruit unless they remain connected to the vine, his disciples must remain in him, as he remains in them. He then speaks the following words, which have come down to us in common usage:

> *"This is my commandment: love one another as I love you. **No one has greater love than this to lay down one's life for one's friends**" (John 15:13).*

Most readers will recognize the above, or similar words, in ceremonies honoring the sacrifices men and women have made over the centuries in the service of their country and brethren. Today, these words can be found on gravestones and memorials throughout the world.

13 The Passion of Jesus Begins

Introduction

The final chapters of the Gospels record the end of Jesus' public ministry, which occurred during the week leading to his crucifixion and death. This is referred to as the "Passion" (See "Introduction" to Section 8, Page 101). Christians celebrate this period as "Holy Week." The major events include: Jesus' Entry into Jerusalem ("Palm Sunday"), "The Cleansing of the Temple,"[89] "The Anointing at Bethany," "The Last Supper," "The Agony in the Garden," "The Trial Before Pontius Pilate," his death, burial and what Christians believe was his "Resurrection." The Gospels tell us that the week began on a Sunday, with Jesus' "triumphal" entry into Jerusalem and that he was crucified and died five days later, on what Christians refer to as "Good Friday." Christian's celebrate Jesus' Resurrection on "Easter Sunday," which also marks the last day of "Lent"[90] for many Christians.

Because of the importance of the last week of Jesus' life to his ministry (its portrayal accounts for almost one-third of the Gospels) a significant portion of this narrative will likewise be devoted to this six-day period. This is necessary to give context to many of the phrases that have come down to us in common usage from this period, and to provide the reader with details and discussion on what is probably the least known and certainly most misunderstood aspects of Jesus' final days, including events such as "The Last Supper," whose commemoration led to the slaughter of countless early Christians by the Romans – who believed the ritual involved cannibalism!

The reader is not asked to accept the account of Jesus rising from the dead, or related passages, and they neither strengthen nor detract from the purpose of this book. The details of these Gospel passages are only intended to provide the reader with an appreciation of what as seen as the primary motivation for Jesus' disciples to carry on his teachings following his death, despite the persecution and martyrdom that many endured because of their belief. That belief has grown into a world-wide following and continues to manifest itself for good up to the present moment.

It is also pertinent to note that there is some variation among the Gospels as to the specific days on which certain events occurred during the final week,[91] but that is not a concern that needs to be addressed, since the Gospels agree on the important details. Also, as noted in the in opening section of this book "Historicity of the Gospels" (Page 26) such apparent differences are to be expected, since the accounts of Jesus' life and teachings were passed on by oral tradition, until they began to be recorded a few decades following his death.

Finally, while the story of Jesus public life and teachings, as entered above, was primarily based on Matthew's Gospel, with entries from the other three Gospels following in turn, the final sections of this narrative will be taken from all four Gospels concurrently, based on the chronological order in which the events occurred.

Jesus' Entry into Jerusalem

Matthew 21:1-9

The last week of Jesus' life commences with Matthew's account of Jesus' "triumphal" entry into Jerusalem, which Christians now celebrate as "Palm Sunday." The term derives from the Gospel's account of a large crowd spreading palm tree branches on the ground as Jesus approached the city. The Gospels also record that the crowd cried out his name as he passed, and shouted:

> *"Hosanna[92]to the Son of David: Blessed is he who comes in the name of the Lord;" (Matthew 21:9)*

While there is no historical record of this event, all four Gospels record it, with many Christian Church's commemorating the event by the distribution of palms as part of Palm Sunday services. Interestingly, the palms can be returned to the church a year later, where they are burned, with their ashes used to bless the congregation at the mass which marks the start of Lent each year. This mass, known as "Ash Wednesday" is celebrated by many Christian denominations as well, and includes the church clergy's placing the ashes on the heads of the participants. The Roman Catholic Church marks a cross on the forehead of each recipient with the ashes, while reciting the words "Remember thou art dust and unto dust thou shalt return" [93] to remind them of their mortality and need to repent of their sins, while there is still time.

The Cleansing of the Temple

Matthew 21:12-17

As was the custom, upon entering Jerusalem Jesus went directly to the Great Temple. He was followed by a large crowd. Incensed at what he sees, Jesus creates bedlam, overturning money changers' tables[94] and flaying merchants who were selling animals for sacrifice, shouting:

> *"It is written: My house shall be a house of prayer, but you are making it a **den of thieves.**"*

The phrase "den of thieves" has been used many times in literature, music, and in media. In 1992 Pulitzer winning author James B. Stewart released the best-selling book *"Den of Thieves,"* which tells the story of an insider-trading scandal that rocked Wall Street.

The Anointing in Bethany

Mark 14:3-7

The anointing of Jesus is another of the events reported in each of the four Gospels. As recorded in both Mark and Matthew, Jesus and his disciples left Jerusalem after spending the first day in the Temple and traveled to the nearby town of Bethany, where they were greeted by an unknown woman at a house at which they were to stay. (She was identified as Mary, sister of Lazarus, in John Chapter 12). As Jesus entered the house the woman took a measure of costly perfumed oil and massaged his feet. Judas Iscariot, the disciple who would later betray Jesus, demanded to know why the oil had not been sold and the money distributed to the poor. Jesus answers Judas with the following words:

> *"Leave her alone. Let her keep this for the day of my burial. **The poor you will always have with you;** but you will not always have me."*

The key to understanding Jesus' response here is to recognize that he is quoting scripture, as he had many times before. Jesus' words here echo Deuteronomy 15:11 "The land will never lack for needy persons."

Jesus' use of the aphorism that being poor is an inherent condition of man can be easily misunderstood, particularly by those who believe that it is the duty of humanity to elevate the poor from their humble status, seemingly as if it were a medical condition. Perhaps, the "poor" might be better served if poverty were treated as a medical condition, so that "preventive medicine" and seeking a "cure" might finally be given the same attention as treating its "symptoms."

Obviously, Jesus' words here were not intended as a disparaging remark, as his compassion for the poor is evident throughout his public ministry; witness his many discourses entered above. Certainly, no one today should doubt this, given the recent words of Pope Francis I, and the life of Mother Teresa of Calcutta.

Not surprisingly, many who had little in the way of material things in their formative years considered themselves as being poor. Indeed, the history of America is written in the stories of immigrants whose hard work not only improved their own condition, but elevated the entire country. There is a wonderful saying the reader may have heard on the subject: "He is rich or poor according to what he is, not according to what he has."[95] Hopefully, we can all agree on the truth of these words.

Jesus Returns to the Temple Each Day
Luke 21:37-38

Luke tells us that Jesus came to the Temple each day to preach and after the first night in Bethany, he stayed at the Mount of Olives at night.[96] Based on the Gospel accounts of Jesus being tried on a Thursday or Friday, it appears that he spent four or five days teaching in the Temple.

Jesus is Questioned by the Chief Priests and Elders

Matthew 21:23-27

Matthew Chapter 21:23-27, gives us another example of the ability of Jesus to confound the religious leaders of the day when confronted with theological questions designed to entrap him. When Jesus returned to the Temple the day following the "cleansing" of it, the Chief Priests and Elders asked him by what "authority" had he acted. If Jesus had replied that the authority had come from God, he would have been condemned for blasphemy; if he had not said this, then he would be guilty of desecrating the Temple, which would also have subject him to condemnation.

Sensing their purpose, Jesus responds by telling them he will answer their question, if they can tell him by what authority had John the Baptist baptized Jews for the forgiveness of sins. Matthew writes that since the people in the Temple were listening to this, the Chief Priests were unsure how to respond, as they knew that many present thought John a great prophet, and the priests were concerned their response could cause a riot. They finally answered that they did not know. Jesus then tells them that since they could not answer his question, he would not answer theirs.

Jesus' response not only denied the Chief Priests and Church Elders a reason to have him arrested, but their inability to respond diminished their authority before the people. Jesus also knew that if they could not recognize that John was a prophet, neither would they recognize his authority. Jesus understood this would always be so and instructed his disciples not to seek the approval of those who were closed to his message. (Matthew 10:14, Page 92.)

Jesus Confronts the Church Elders

Matthew 21:33-46

Here Matthew describes Jesus' use of parables to chastise the Chief Priests, Pharisees, and Church Elders[97] for their treatment of the common people. Matthew writes that Jesus knew that this would lead to the Sanhedrin's[98] decision to have him arrested. In Matthew 21:42 Jesus tells the Church Elders that the common people would enter heaven before they would, quoting Psalm 118:22:

> *"Did you never read in the scriptures: '**The stone that the builders rejected has become the cornerstone;**[99] by the Lord has this been done, and it is wonderful in our eyes?'"*

Jesus was obviously using "cornerstone" as a metaphor for himself and his ministry, which he knew would be rejected by the Church Elders. The reference to the importance of the "cornerstone" is as timely as any of Jesus' proverbs and parables.

Jesus Continues to Confront Church Elders

Matthew 22:1-14

Jesus continues confronting the Church Elders with parables, one containing a veiled warning about a king who sent his servants to summon guests to a wedding feast for his son, but none came, even after the king had sent his servants a second time. The king takes revenge upon those who so dishonored him, sending his servants to the main roads to invite whoever they find to attend the feast, while condemning those originally invited to harsh punishment, using a phrase many may recognize:

> ***"There will be wailing and grinding of teeth"*** *(Matthew 22:13).*

This phrase appears many times and in various forms in the New Testament as a reference to the torments of hell. The one familiar to most is "there shall be weeping and gnashing of teeth." It has become a well-used idiomatic expression in colloquial English and can be found in works of art and literature and even in music.

Jesus concludes the parable with words that are repeated throughout the Gospels, albeit in differing form.

> *"Many are invited, but few are chosen" (Matthew 22:14).*

Jesus uses opposing terms here to dramatize his message, as was done in "The Beatitudes" (See Page 64). The technique is referred to as "antithesis," from the Greek for "setting opposite." There have been many famous examples outside the Gospels, including in the 1961 inaugural given by John F. Kennedy, alluded to above.

Payment of Taxes to the Emperor
Matthew 22:15-22

In a further attempt to entrap Jesus, the Church Elders ask him if it is legal to pay taxes to the Romans. Jesus' answer is so compelling that the writer included it in the opening sections of this book. (Matthew 22:15, Page 52) Jesus' response concluded with the now famous words:

> *"Then repay to Caesar what belongs to Caesar and to God what belongs to God."*

The reason for the reintroduction of this passage here is to lend context and depth to Jesus' amazing response, since it took place amid a series of exchanges with the Church Elders in the Temple area in Jerusalem, which would insure that there would be many witnesses to his answer. Since the city was also the seat of the Roman authority in Judea, the Church officials were sure that they had trapped Jesus; he would have no choice but to violate the Jewish Law if he endorsed the payment of tribute to the Romans, or be the recipient of their sure and swift justice, should he advocate otherwise.

Jesus Explains the Resurrection, Calling on God's Words
Matthew 22:23-33

The Church Elders follow by asking Jesus to explain his teaching about the Resurrection. While the Old Testament contains accounts of prophets raising the dead,[100] the Elders question Jesus' teaching that all mankind will rise from the dead in a final judgment. They sought to make this belief seem absurd by asking Jesus if a woman had married seven brothers in succession after each had died, whose wife would she be at the Resurrection. Jesus answers by saying *"none,"* since the marital relationship would not survive death. Jesus also calls on God's words and declares:

> *"And concerning the Resurrection of the dead, have you not read what was said to you by God, 'I am the God of Abraham, the God of Isaac, and the God of Jacob?'[101] He is not the God of the dead but of the living" (Matthew 22:31-32).*

The Gospels contain more than one passage which records Jesus raising someone who had died. Christians view Jesus' raising a dear friend Lazarus from the dead as central to their faith. In John Chapter 11, Lazarus' sister Martha tells Jesus that she knows she will see her brother, who had died three days earlier, rise at the time of the final resurrection. Jesus tells her she will see him sooner, using words that are seen by many Christians among the most profound of all those recorded in the Gospels; Jesus becomes the **destroyer of death:**

> *"I am the Resurrection and the life; whoever believes in me, even if he dies, will live, and everyone who lives and believes in me will never die." (John 11:25-26).*

Finally, since Christians see Jesus' resurrection as the single most important event in human history, it is altogether fitting to include pertinent Gospel passages describing Jesus' trial, death and resurrection in the final sections of this book, and role they played in the rise of Jesus' prominence following his brief life and ignominious death.

The Second Greatest Commandment
Matthew 22:34-40

When the Pharisees learned that Jesus had *"silenced the Sadducees"* with his answers regarding their attempt to show his teachings were heretical, one of them was chosen to test Jesus further. This *"scholar of the Law" (Matthew 22:35)* asked Jesus which of God's commandments was the *"greatest?"*

Jesus response echoes a familiar theme found throughout the Gospels:

> *"You shall love the Lord, your God, with all your heart, with all your soul, and with all your mind. This is the greatest and the first commandment. The second is like it:* ***You shall love your neighbor as yourself.*** *The whole law and the prophets depend on these two commandments."*

In the first part of the passage entered above Jesus is quoting from Deuteronomy 6:5, which is the first of the Ten Commandments given to Moses[102] by God, which many believe is the basis for all Mosaic law. The second "Commandment" that Jesus quoted is from Leviticus 19:18.

This second "Commandment" is truly remarkable, in that it places the love of one's fellow man above all other commandments, save for the love of God. While the Old Testament commandment was meant for members of the Jewish faith, Jesus' response was meant for all of humankind, for when asked to define who was their *"neighbor,"* he responded with the parable of The Good Samaritan, (Luke 10:29-37, Page 119) who clearly represented any man.

Jesus Denounces the Scribes and Pharisees for the Last Time

Matthew 23:1-39

On the final day that Jesus would come to the Temple, he unloosed a series of denunciations of the Scribes and Pharisees that must have been the last straw, as the combined group of the Church Elders, Scribes, Pharisees and Sadducees thereafter met and planned to have Jesus arrested and put to death. The denunciations are described as the "Seven Woes" or "Woes of the Pharisees.," as Jesus repeatedly used the term *"Woe to you,"* as he denounced them as hypocrites and liars, calling them serpents and a ***"brood of vipers."*** *(Matthew 23:33)*

The term "viper's brood" was a commonly used expression at the time of Jesus, used to describe those who were perceived as being filled with malice. This verse has been used by more than a few famous writers, including William Shakespeare in *Troilus and Cressida*, Anthony Trollope in *Barchester Towers*, and W. Somerset Maugham in *Catalina*, and was included in the title of a book by one of France's celebrated authors, François Mauriac.

14 Jesus' Final Teachings to His Disciples

Introduction

Jesus' final teachings and instructions to his disciples occurred while they were staying at the Mount of Olives following his teaching in the Temple during the day. He spoke to them using many parables, some of which were recorded earlier in this text, such as the story of the Faithful Servant (Luke 12:35, Page 123). While the other three Gospels record these events, this section will record them as entered in Matthew Chapters 24 and 25.

The "Olivet Prophecy"

Matthew 24:3-36

Matthew reports that following another confrontation with the religious leaders at the Temple, Jesus went out of the city to the Mount of Olives. As he is leaving the Temple area he turns and tells his Apostles.

> *"You see all these things, do you not? Amen, I say to you, there will not be left here a stone upon another stone that will not be thrown down."*

Jesus prediction that the Great Temple would be destroyed in the lifetime of the Apostles came to pass about 40 years after he was crucified. Jesus also told his Apostles that they will suffer many trials and persecutions and foretold the ending of the world, which was described as the Tribulation.* This Chapter became known as the "Olivet Prophecy," because of the location where the last of Jesus' five discourses took place. Many of the parables Jesus used were repeated from earlier teachings to his disciples, probably to insure that they were understood and remembered. The most salient ones were entered earlier.

The Parable of the Ten Virgins
Matthew 25:1-13

One of the parables Jesus employed while instructing his disciples has been referred to as the "Parable of the Ten Virgins." Here Jesus tells a story about ten virgins awaiting the appearance of their bridegrooms.[103] While five were wise and had prepared by having additional flasks of oil available, five were foolish and did not have enough oil to keep their lamps lit. When the foolish virgins' oil was consumed, they left to buy more and were absent when the groom returned, prompting one of Jesus' more familiar phrases:

> *"Therefore, stay awake, for you know neither the day nor the hour" (Matthew 25:13).*

Jesus is clearly petitioning his disciples to keep their eye on the ball and at the same time reminding all of us to give attention to the things in our lives that matter. The message here is as timely as any of Jesus' teachings, as none of us truly knows when we will draw our last breath. Many sayings and traditions have arisen based on this truth, including "do not let the sun set on your anger." (Ephesians 4:26).

The reader may recall a scene from the critically acclaimed

---

* Some biblical scholars have interpreted Jesus' prophecy of tribulation to refer to the destruction of the Temple in Jerusalem in AD 70.

movie *The Shawshank Redemption*, wherein the warden, played by Bob Gunton, goes to the cell of the convicted banker Andy Dufrense (played by Tim Robbins) and is gratified to see that Andy has a copy of the Bible. The warden asks Andy what his favorite passage was, to which he replies, "Watch therefore, for ye know neither the day nor the hour" (Matthew 25:13 KJV). Prophetically, Andy later escapes and exposes the warden's many crimes, which results in his committing suicide at the moment of his arrest.

There is a parallel to Jesus' words here; it is part of an inspirational prayer that the famed Alabama Football Coach Paul W. "Bear" Bryant reportedly carried in his wallet. It read, in part, "What I do today is important because I am exchanging one day of my life for it." And if we knew today was to be our last, how would we spend it, and who among us would trade away one day of our lives, if it were a commodity that could be bartered?

The Parable of the Ten Talents

Matthew 25:14-30

Here, Jesus tells his Apostles a parable of rich man who before going on a journey calls his servants to him and entrusts them with his wealth. He gives five talents[104] to one, three to another, and one to the third, according to their station. After a long time, he returns and finds that the first two servants had invested his money wisely, increasing his wealth, and rewards each, accordingly. However, the third servant had simply stored the talent, explaining he had not invested it for fear of it losing value. (Something to which we all can relate) Upon hearing this, the master rebukes the servant and casts him into the dark, saying:

> *"You knew that I harvest where I did not plant and gather where I did not scatter?"*

While the parable appears to be calling his disciples to a life of proselytization[105] using their God-given "talents," it can be applied to any form of stewardship and calls to mind another of Jesus' passages which counsels that to whom much is given, much will be required. (Luke 12:48, Page 123)

This parable has been the subject of paintings, including one by Rembrandt, and has been used in literature as well. It appears as a common theme in the writings of the great English poet John Milton, whose *Paradise Lost* is regarded as one of greatest works in literature. The renowned American sociologist and Columbia University professor Robert King Merton also used it in one of his famous articles.[106]

15 The Last Supper

Introduction

The Last Supper," or what Catholics celebrate as "Holy Communion," is the central part of Christians' religious services, and is perhaps the most misunderstood of all of the traditions that have come down to us from Jesus' teachings. The event marked the start of the Jewish Passover celebration which is observed with the traditional meal, or Seder, of unleavened bread, bitter herbs, roasted lamb and wine, each course accompanied by the recital of traditional prayers. The ceremony celebrated the Jews' freedom from bondage in Egypt. During the meal Jesus told his Apostles that one among them is going to betray him. The meal concluded with Jesus leading his Apostles back to the Mount of Olives for the night which dawned with his arrest, an event that was to become known as the "Agony in the Garden."

The Betrayal of Jesus by Judas

Matthew 26:14-16

As noted earlier, while Jesus was teaching in the Temple, the Church leaders met and decided to have him tried and put to death. Since they were concerned that arresting Jesus while he was teaching in the Temple could lead to a serious incident should his many followers try to prevent it, they sent word that anyone who reported where Jesus was staying at night would receive a reward. Upon learning this, Judas Iscariot went to the

Chief Priests; the meeting is recorded as follows:

> *"What are you willing to give me if I hand him over to you?* ***They paid him thirty pieces of silver****, and from that time on he looked for an opportunity to hand him over." (Matthew 26:15).*

While there has been significant debate as to Judas' motives, the act has come down to us as the definition of treachery; in fact, the very word "Judas" is still synonymous with the act of betrayal, in some quarters. The thirty pieces of silver paid by the Chief Priests, which was the sum traditionally paid at that time for a man with a price on his head, has also become a phrase employed for the act of selling out one's principles or ideals for material gain. In addition, since Judas represented the thirteenth person present at the Last Supper, the aversion to the number 13, while predating this, became prevalent in popular culture because of the Gospels' recounting of what was to follow Judas' betrayal.

"The Last Supper"
Matthew 26:26-30

The Gospels tell us that Jesus and his disciples celebrated the start of Passover at sundown on the day before his arrest. Because of the significance to all Christians of Jesus' words at the time of this event, it is hoped that the reader will find its description enlightening. Certainly, there is enough controversy and misconception surrounding it to warrant some discussion here. While many non-Christians may be familiar with the Gospel accounts of the Last Supper, it is hoped that the following will help the reader to more fully understand the significance to Christians, and their observance of it as the central part of their religious observances.

When the Apostles were reclining at the Seder table, Jesus told them that one among them would betray him. While they are searching one another's countenances, Jesus identifies the betrayer as Judas, who immediately leaves. Matthew continues:

> *While they were eating, Jesus took bread, said the blessing, broke it, and giving it to his disciples said,* ***'Take and eat; this is my body.'***
>
> *Then he took a cup, gave thanks, and gave it to them, saying,* ***'Drink from it, all of you, for this is my blood of the covenant,***[107] *which will be shed on behalf of many for the forgiveness of sins.' (Matthew 26:30).*

Jesus' words here were meant to both seal the new covenant he has given to his Apostles and symbolize the offering of himself as a sacrifice for the forgiveness of sins. In Luke 22:19 Jesus tells his disciples:

> *"Do this in memory of me."*[108]

Jesus' words here are easily the most remarkable and controversial of all those recorded in the Gospels. While Jesus had previously told many that he was the "Bread of Life" (John 6:22-59, Page 129), this is the first time he talks about himself in this manner; and while the use of blood was integral to Jewish sacrificial rites and their sealing of a covenant to obey God's laws,[109] the drinking of it was, and remains, strictly forbidden by Jewish law.

Not surprisingly, Jesus' words sparked a huge controversy among his followers and led to his rejection by many Jews. Moreover, one of the reasons early Christians were persecuted by the Romans is the belief that the celebration of Mass involved cannibalism. Of significance, historians of antiquity view matters of this nature as supportive of the validity of the event, since it is doubtful that anyone would invent something so controversial and frankly extraordinary.

The Agony in the Garden - Jesus is Arrested
Matthew 26:36-56

When the meal was completed Jesus and his disciples went back to the mount of olives. There Jesus goes off to pray alone. His fears of capture are revealed as he asks God to save him from the agony he knows is sure to follow when he is taken. His anxiety is heightened as he finds his disciples sleeping and, upon waking Peter, he says to him: "*So you could not keep watch with me for one hour? . . .* ***the spirit is willing, but the flesh is weak***" (Matthew 26:40-41). With that Judas arrives with the temple guards and others and kisses Jesus in greeting, which was the signal arranged for identifying him in the dark. When one of the servants of the high priest lays hands on Jesus, Peter strikes the man's head with a sword, prompting Jesus to say one of the more recognized phrases from the Gospels:

> *Then Jesus said to him, "Put your sword back into its sheath,* ***for all who take the sword will perish by the sword."*** *(Matthew 26:52)*

These words have come down to us as "those who live by the sword shall die by the sword" and reflects the belief that violence begets violence. The allegory can be found in one form or other in many of the world's religions.

16 Jesus is Tried and Condemned

Introduction

While Matthew's Gospel provided a substantial accounting of the early ministry and initial events following Jesus' entry into Jerusalem, the Gospels of Mark, John, and Luke provide details of the last week of his life that are not recorded in depth in Matthew. Accordingly, passages from all four Gospels will be used to complete this narrative.

The reader may again ask what teachings of Jesus can be gained from the details of his arrest, trial, crucifixion, and death. However, as stated in the Introduction to section 13 above, it is hoped that the reader will benefit by their inclusion since they both provide context to sayings contained within the passages which have come down to us in our everyday usage, such as "I wash my hands of this" and provide the reader with background to better understand the amazing growth of Christianity following Jesus' death.

Jesus is Brought Before the Sanhedrin[110]

Matthew 26:57-68

The Gospels tell us that when Jesus was arrested he was bound, blindfolded, mocked, and severely beaten as he was dragged to a hastily arranged meeting of the Sanhedrin and their High Priest Caiaphas, where he was *"examined."* Jesus remained silent as witnesses testified against him, finally prompting the High Priest to rise and say:

> *"I order you to tell us under oath before the living God whether you are the Messiah, the Son of God.*

Jesus replied,

> ***"You have said so."*** *(Matthew 26:63-64)*

The High Priest thereupon tore his robes and said:

> *"He has blasphemed! What further need have we of witnesses?" (Matthew 26:65).*

Then Caiaphas asked the assemblage for their *"opinion"*; they answered:

> *"He deserves to die!" (Matthew 26:66)*

The next morning, Jesus was bound and taken to Pontius Pilate, the Roman prefect of Judea, where he is accused of sedition for claiming he is the king of the Jews.

The Sanhedrin apparently decided to turn Jesus over to the Romans out of concern for the reaction of his followers, should they attempt to have him put to death. They knew Roman Law well and the fact that Rome only recognized the authority of the emperor, and anyone claiming to be a king would immediately be sentenced to death. They calculated that the spectacle of a public execution by the Romans would ensure the acquiescence of Jesus' followers.

Judas Deeply Regrets Betraying Jesus
Matthew 27:3-10

When Judas learns that Jesus has been condemned, he deeply regrets what he has done and returns to the Temple to give the thirty pieces of silver back to the priests. When they refuse to accept the return of the ransom money, Judas flings the coins into the Temple and goes out and hangs himself. The Temple priests agree they cannot keep this "blood money" and decide to use it to purchase a burial place for foreigners, which became known as "potter's field"* (Matthew 27:7).

Jesus is Brought Before Pontius Pilate
Luke 23:1-7

Luke reports that the entire assembly of the Sanhedrin brought Jesus before Pilate and charged him with crimes against Rome by opposing the payment of taxes to Caesar, and claiming he is the Messiah, a king. When Jesus is questioned by Pilate, he remains silent, except to say, when asked if he is a king he replies:

> *"My kingdom does not belong to this world." John 18:36*

Not wishing to condemn Jesus, who is a Galilean, he tells the Sanhedrin that he finds no fault with Jesus and sends him to Herod, Tetrarch of Galilee, as he has the first jurisdiction.

Pilate Sends Jesus to Herod Antipas
Luke 23:6-11

While this passage is only found in Luke, Pilate's attempts to avoid condemning Jesus are found in all four Gospels, which could logically include his sending Jesus to Herod Antipas for trial. While Luke reports that Herod questioned Jesus at length, he gave no answer, whereupon Herod returned Jesus to Pilate, seemingly eager to avoid the trouble that plagued him following

---

* The term "potter's field" referred to a plot of land that contained a large amount of clay, used to make pottery, but useless for agriculture. From that time on, the term has become synonymous with any graveyard used to bury the poor.

the beheading of John the Baptist (Matthew 14:3, Page 98).

Jesus is Returned to Pontius Pilate
Luke 23:11-16

When Jesus is again brought before Pilate, he summoned the Chief Priests, Church officials and the people and said to them:

"You brought this man to me and accused him of inciting the people to revolt. I have conducted my investigation in your presence and have not found this man guilty of the charges you have brought against him, nor did Herod, for he sent him back to me. Therefore, I shall have him flogged and then release him."

Despite the exhortations of the Sanhedrin and other Church officials, Pilate clearly did not want to condemn Jesus who, by that time, had a large following. He knew well the unrest of the population under Roman rule and would have wished to avoid stroking their rebellious nature, particularly, since he had to have known that he was being used to punish someone because of dissenting religious views.

The Crowd Shouts for Jesus to be Crucified
Matthew 27:18-26

Pilate continues to seek a way to avoid condemning Jesus by offering to free him, as it was the custom for the Romans to release a condemned prisoner during Passover. However, the gathered crowd called for a notorious prisoner named Barabbas to be released, instead. When Pilate saw the crowd was near to rioting, he relented and turned Jesus over to be crucified, after performing a ritual to make it clear he was absolving himself of the decision:

> ***"He took water and washed his hands in the sight of the crowd, saying, 'I am innocent of this man's***

blood. Look to it yourselves'" *(Mt. 27:24).*

While the act of washing one's hands to become free of guilt may have first been recorded in the Old Testament (Dt.21:6), the Gospel's accounting of this event popularized the common phrase "I wash my hands of it." Today, it is employed to signify one's denial of responsibility for something likely to bring censure. The words found their way into Shakespeare's *Richard III (Act I, Scene IV)* and the symbolism of Pilate's act appears to have played a role in Shakespeare's *Macbeth.* After plotting the death of Duncan with her husband Macbeth, Lady Macbeth is later seen compulsively washing her hands to cleanse an imagined stain *(Act V, scene I).*

It is altogether fitting here to discuss Christianity's wrongful persecution of Jews, who were blamed for Jesus' death, even unto today in some quarters. However, while many of the church Elders at the time were willing participants in Jesus' trial and execution, Christianity itself started out as a Jewish religious order, and virtually all of Jesus' disciples and early followers were themselves Jews! Forgetting the fact that his teachings call for Christians to be tolerant and forgiving, Jesus made it clear that he held no one responsible for his crucifixion saying "*. . . I lay down my life in order to take it up again. No one takes it from me, but I lay it down on my own.*" (Jn. 10:17-18) Despite this, and the early promulgations of Papal Bulls obligating Christians to protect Jews, some so-called "Christians" continue to harbor hatred for Jews in the insane belief that they are somehow responsible for the acts of a few of their remote ancestors. The absurdity of this could not be more apparent.

17 The Crucifixion of Jesus

Introduction

Most of us are familiar with the Gospel accounts of Jesus' crucifixion, which was the Roman method of public execution for crimes calling for the capital punishment; it was primarily used for slaves and enemies of the state. The practice is well documented in historical records and was designed as a gruesome, degrading, and excruciatingly painful death, both to punish the criminal and to terrify witnesses to deter them from similar crimes or dissent. (Interestingly. the word "excruciating" comes from the word "crucifixion.") Christians believe that Jesus was crucified on the Friday of the Passion Week, referred to as "Good Friday."

The purpose of the entry of the details of Jesus' Crucifixion, which event was recorded by historians,* is done primarily to address those who have questioned whether Jesus survived the crucifixion, to later appear as if he had risen from dead. Also, to have omitted an event so important to Christians would have been remiss, given the impact upon the future of mankind, both

* As mentioned earlier, there is near universal agreement among scholars of antiquity that Jesus was crucified under Pontius Pilate. The practice, including scourging, and the nailing of the hands and feet to the cross is well documented, and the resultant injuries are consistent with the forensic examination of the image contained on Shroud of Turin, which will be discussed briefly below, due to the continued interest in it.

positive and, all too often, otherwise.

Jesus is Scourged

(John 19:1-3)

Jesus' Crucifixion was preceded by a scourging[111] by the Roman guards shortly after sunrise, or about 6:30 AM.* The practice was done to punish the accused and to hasten death, when such was wanted. As entered above, since the Romans knew that Jesus had a large following, the sight of a scourged Jesus' would have been a way to both dampen the fervor of the crowds which were sure to follow, and insure his speedy death and burial.

Scourging was accomplished with Roman *flagrum* which was a whip composed of a handle fitted with multiple leather straps whose ends were fastened with rough iron balls and pieces of bone, designed to tear the flesh. The damage to the body was severe, with the loss of large amounts of blood, accompanied by the early onset of shock.

Jesus is Made to Carry the Cross

John 19-17

Typically, once the Romans completed scourging the condemned, they would be forced to carry a cross[112] to the place of execution, typically outside the walls of the city.[113] This location was generally chosen to serve as a graphic warning to anyone entering or leaving a city. While carrying the cross the Gospels tell us that Jesus fell three times, the scourging having left him in a seriously weakened state. After falling for the third time, the

---

* It is probable that the Romans started the scourging very early that day so the crucifixion could be completed before noon, with the expectation that Jesus would be dead before dark to allow for his burial by nightfall, as required by Jewish law.

Gospels tell us that the guards enlisted a bystander to carry the cross to the place of execution. It can be presumed that Jesus reached the place of execution by mid-morning.

Jesus is Crucified

John 19:23-34

The Gospels tell us that once Jesus reached the place of execution he was stripped naked and nailed to the cross.[114] This would have intensified the pain and the trauma upon his body, further hastening his death. The crucifixion itself would have been carried out by a team of four specially trained Roman soldiers, commanded by a Centurion.

It also was the practice of the Romans to break the legs of the condemned, but John's Gospel states that when the guards went to do this, they found Jesus was already dead. Because Roman guards were prohibited from leaving until death was certain, the Gospels' account of what followed is credible:

> *But when they came to Jesus and saw that he was already dead, they did not break his legs, but one soldier thrust his lance into his side, and immediately blood and water flowed out.*

The significance of this Gospel entry has only recently come to light, as water flowing from a wound in the body cavity (a clear fluid that collects around the heart and lungs prior to death) could only result from a puncture of the heart and lung membranes,[115] something unknown to people of Jesus' era. While not offering proof of Jesus' death upon the cross, this entry in the Gospels adds authenticity to their accounts of Jesus' crucifixion and the piercing of Jesus' lungs and heart to insure his death.

18 The Death of Jesus

Introduction

As outlined above, the Gospels record that the scourging and crucifixion of Jesus were completed before noon on the Friday of the week,* and that Jesus died some three to six hours later, depending on differing Gospel accounts. According to forensic studies of the effect of scourging and crucifixion upon the body, Jesus' death could readily have occurred in a matter of hours due to a number of serious medical conditions, any one of which could have been fatal – including loss of blood, hypoventilation-induced acidosis, exhaustive asphyxia,[116] cardiac arrest, pulmonary embolism, dehydration, and other medical conditions.

Jesus' Last Words

Matthew 27:45-50

While the Gospels give differing accounts of Jesus' last words, Matthew and Mark record what scholars of antiquity consider the most historically supportable:

> *"E'li, E'li, la'ma sa ·bach ·tha'ni?," which is Aramaic for "My God, My God, why have you forsaken me?" (Matthew 27:46 and Mark 15:34)*

---

* The Gospels further described how Jesus was severely beaten when arrested and during his "examination" before the Sanhedrin. This, coupled with an obvious lack of sleep, water, and food after the "Last Supper", would have left Jesus in a seriously weakened state, even before the scourging and crucifixion took place.

The authenticity of the Gospels' inclusion of these words is supported by the "Criterion of Embarrassment" which holds that an author would not have invented something that would have embarrassed the early Church, as would be the case in the portrayal of Jesus uttering that he had been abandoned by God. However, some biblical scholars believe Jesus was reciting a line from Psalm 22, the reading of which would lead to a far different understanding of Jesus' last words.

The Earth Shook and the Skies Darkened
Matthew 27:51 and Luke 23:44

Another detail that supports the Gospels' accounts of the death of Jesus can be found in the writings of the secular Greek historian Phlegon, who lived in the second century, and the Greek Historian Thallus, whose account some scholars believe dates to within twenty years of Jesus' crucifixion. According to records from the time,[117] the sky darkened and earthquakes occurred around the time of Jesus' death. The inclusion of these facts is only intended to add to the credibility of the Gospels' entries, whether these events are viewed as meteorological, geophysical, or otherwise.

19 The Burial of Jesus

Introduction

The Gospels tell us that a wealthy and respected Pharisee, Joseph of Arimathea, asked for and received Pilate's permission for Jesus to be buried before the Jewish Sabbath, which began at sundown that evening. The Romans removed the body from the cross and gave it to Joseph, who had it wrapped in linen (the Shroud of Turin?) and laid in a nearby tomb that had been hewn in rock. The Gospels report that the Romans placed a large stone in front of the tomb, as was the practice of the day, and on the order of Pilate, stood watch, as the Jewish Elders were concerned that Jesus' followers would remove his body and claim he had risen, as he had prophesied.

The Burial Cloth – The Shroud of Turin?

Matthew 27:57-60

For those who are interested, the "Shroud of Turin" (the "Shroud") is a length of woven linen fabric some Christians believe is the burial cloth of Jesus; the Roman Catholic Church considers the Shroud a holy relic but makes no claim as to its origin. The Shroud bears the faint image of a crucified man first discovered on a photographic negative taken by an Italian amateur photographer in 1898. The Shroud has resided in the Cathedral of Saint John the Baptist in Turin, Italy since 1578; hence its name. Since the time of its discovery, the Shroud has been the subject of intense debate by both the religious and scientific community. The most significant argument against its authenticity is based on radiocarbon tests done in 1988 which place the age of the shroud to a medieval period between AD 1260–1390.

More recently, a tomb discovered in Jerusalem in 2009, and dating to the time Jesus, contained a burial cloth whose composition was taken as evidence that the Shroud of Turin could not have been the burial cloth of Jesus.

Regarding the radiocarbon dating, an article published in the *Wall Street Journal* on April 18, 2015 reports that more than a few scientists who have examined the available physical evidence have called for additional scientific testing, based on the possibility that centuries of handling and other events, such as fire damage, may have affected the radiocarbon dating of the very small sampling which was used in the testing.

Regarding the 2009 discovery, a 2010 report published by the *International Workshop on the Scientific Approach to Acheiropoietos Images* repudiates the conclusions drawn in a 2009 report.[118] Moreover, there are many amazing facts about the shroud that science cannot explain, as well as possible proofs of the existence of the shroud dating to hundreds of years prior to the age established by the radiocarbon dating.

One thing is certain, if the shroud is a forgery it was fashioned by some medieval conjuror whose scientific, medical, and historical knowledge of the subject, as well as creative talents and technological skills exceed modern science's ability to explain or duplicate.

20 The Resurrection of Jesus

Introduction

Since belief in the resurrection of Jesus is at the center of Christian faith,* a discourse on his life and teachings would not be complete if this event were omitted. However, since there is no historical evidence to support this "miracle," it is only reasonable to question what evidence we have that it occurred. Logic leads one to question if it were possible for Jesus to somehow have survived the crucifixion (which is an historical fact), or for his disciples to have hidden his body and later claim he had risen.†

To consider the first point, there is historical proof that Jesus was crucified by the Romans, and there are ample records which show that the Romans were experts at this form of execution. We know too that, aside from the well-known discipline of the Roman soldier, those charged with carrying out such sentences would themselves be subject to a similar fate, should they fail to ensure the death of the condemned. Further, since it was well-known that Jesus had prophesized that he would rise from the dead, those who wanted him executed would have sent trusted

---

* As Saint Paul said, "And if Christ has not been raised, then empty is our preaching; empty, too, your faith." (1 Cor. 15:14).

† If the reader has no interest in this discussion please skip to the next chapter and accept the author's apologies for its entry.

members to witness his execution and death. Given these facts, and the extreme nature of the physical mutilation which scourging and crucifixion would have done to the body, along with the piercing of his heart and lungs with a spear, it is it highly unlikely that Jesus somehow survived the crucifixion.

Regarding the possibility that his followers hid his body so they could claim he had risen, again the facts we have appear to indicate otherwise. Firstly, we know that the Apostles were simple, uneducated men who only knew Jesus for a short time, and were only told by Jesus to expect his death, shortly before he was crucified. Not surprisingly, the Gospels tell us the unflattering story of how his followers fled after he was arrested; even Peter, when recognized, denied knowing Jesus (Luke 22:54-61). The Gospels further tell us that only Jesus' mother Mary and a few other women had the courage to witness his crucifixion (Matthew 27:55-56). As set forth on Page 28, above, the "Criterion of Embarrassment" the inclusion of such demeaning statements in the Gospels is viewed as affirming their credibility.

However, his Apostles did not remain in hiding for long; soon after his crucifixion, they came forth and proclaimed that Jesus had risen, and thereafter devoted the remainder of their lives to spreading his word throughout the Mediterranean region, eventually to the far reaches of the Roman Empire and beyond. That neither the Jews nor the Romans took kindly to their movement is an historical fact. The Apostles were ostracized wherever they went and were eventually put to death, along with hundreds of early converts.

Who among us can conceive why any of Jesus' Apostles would leave their family and friends and sacrifice their lives living in foreign lands, only to suffer an agonizing death in the end, if they weren't sure that Jesus had risen? Human nature being what it is, surely at least one of eleven would have revealed an awful truth, if there had been one, in a moment of weakness, or while being tortured. Had this happened, why would any of the other Apostles have remained committed to a lie? Moreover, why would they want to send so many to their deaths at the hands of the Romans for accepting their faith? It is in this light that the narrative of the resurrection of Jesus is entered, hereunder.

The Empty Tomb - Jesus Appears to His Apostles
Luke 24:1-35

All four Gospels contain accounts of Jesus' followers going to the tomb where Jesus was buried on the morning after the Sabbath (Easter Sunday) and, finding the tomb empty, ran to tell the others that the tomb was empty. The Gospels also contain accounts of Jesus appearing to his disciples, seemingly out of nowhere.

Doubting Thomas
John 20:24-29)

The Apostle Thomas was not present when Jesus first appeared to the disciples. When the others' told Thomas of Jesus' visit, he refused to believe them, saying that unless he put his finger into Jesus' wounds he would not believe. When Jesus again appeared to the disciples, Thomas was present and is told by Jesus to put his finger into the nail marks in his hands and place his hand into his side. Whereupon Thomas responds, *"My Lord and My God,"* Hearing this Jesus says:

> *"Have you come to believe because you have seen me? **Blessed are those who have not seen and have believed."***

Jesus' words here underscore the modern dilemma we all face: If God exists, why doesn't he manifest himself clearly, so we may all come to believe?[119] However, if there is an all-knowing and powerful God, he knows that faith, like love, does not come because we wish it; it comes by forces that are beyond our control and are part of the human condition, and would not condemn those who do not believe in him. In the end, it doesn't matter if we believe or not; what matters is how we live our lives. And as Mahatma Gandhi once said, Jesus is the perfect model.

The Commissioning of the Disciples
Matthew 28:16-20

Matthew's final Chapter tells us that at the time of Jesus' last appearance to his Apostles, he commissioned them to follow in his footsteps and continue his ministry with the following words:

> *"Go, therefore, and make disciples of all nations, baptizing them in the name of the Father, and of the Son, and of the Holy Spirit,* [120] *teaching them to observe all that I have commanded you. And behold, I am with you always, until the end of the age."*

Indeed, Jesus' words and actions remain with us today, almost two thousand years after they were uttered to members of a small impoverished community in a remote area of the world.

21 The Ministry of Jesus Continues

Jesus' Ministry is Taken Up by the Apostles and Early Converts

Following Jesus' commissioning of the eleven Apostles, they began to preach throughout Judea and the Roman Empire, including Rome, where Peter was martyred. Early and important converts included Saul of Tarsus (Saint Paul), a Jew and Roman citizen who was to write fourteen of the twenty-seven books of what Catholics accept as the New Testament. Paul's most famous writing is undoubtedly 1 Corinthians 13, which is as well-known to Christians as the Twenty-Third Psalm is to Jews.

Another of Christianity's important early converts Licinius, later known as Saint Luke, who was a Syrian/Greek physician and reportedly a disciple of Paul. Luke wrote both the Gospel and the Acts of the Apostles.

Tradition and historical records tell us that all of Jesus' Apostles (except John), and many of the early converts, were executed by the Romans or Jews. The greatest persecution occurred under orders of the Roman emperor Nero, who claimed that Christians had started the fire that destroyed Rome in the year AD 64. This persecution lasted until the religion was legalized by the emperors Constantine and Licinius in the year AD 313. Many famous converts, including the Emperor Constantine, followed and Christianity became and remains the largest religious following in the world.

Jesus' Ministry Grows into a Worldwide Following

From its early formation to its rise to prominence, Jesus' mission is seen by Christians as continuing throughout the world daily, whether in innumerable works of charity, the parochial/nonsectarian education of youth, the championing of the rights of the underprivileged, caring for the old, sick, and infirm, and calling all of us to a higher moral ground.

While Christianity has received many well-deserved black eyes since Jesus passed the torch, no one can doubt that a discussion of the good that has been done in his name would fill volumes. This was discussed on Page 31, "Jesus' Influence on Humanity."

Other Common Expressions from the New Testament

Beyond the common words and phrases that have come down to us in the four Gospels, the other twenty-three books that make up what Roman Catholics refer to as the New Testament have given rise to many other phrases that will be familiar to the reader. They are listed here with their sources.

"The quick and the dead" (Acts 10:42; 1 Pt. 4:5)

"It is better to give than to receive" (Acts 20:35)

"A law unto themselves" (Rom. 2:14)

"The powers that be" (Rom. 13:1)

"Through a glass darkly" (1 Cor. 13:12)

"Flesh and blood" (1 Cor. 15:50; Eph. 6:12)

"A thorn in my side" (2 Cor. 12:7)

"Thank God" (Rom. 7:21; 1 Cor. 1:14; 2 Tm. 1:3)

"Twinkling of an eye" (1 Cor. 15:52)

"Suffer fools gladly" (2 Cor. 11:19)

"Do not let the sun go down on your wrath" (Eph. 4:26)

"Tenderhearted" (Eph. 4:32)

"Have you in my heart" (Phil. 1:7)

"Labor of love" (1 Thes. 1:3)

"Busybodies" (2 Thes. 3:11; 1 Tm. 5:13)

"Filthy lucre" [slang for money] (1 Tm. 3:3)

"For we brought nothing into the world, just as we shall not be able to take anything out of it" (1 Tm. 6:7)

"The King of Kings" (1 Tm. 6:15; Rv. 17:14; 19:16)

"Fight the good fight" (1 Tm. 6:12)

"The patience of Job" (Jas. 5:11)

"Wallowing in the mire" (2 Pt. 2:22)

"The book of life" (Rv. 3:5))

"Lukewarm" (Rv. 3:16)

"Armageddon" (Rv. 16:16)

"Morning star" (Rv. 22:16).

Postscript

The purpose of writing this book was to illuminate Jesus' teachings, and address issues which have arisen because his followers have frankly failed to follow them on too many occasions. The success (or failure) of this book will not reside in whether the reader comes to believe in Jesus' divinity, but rather in their acceptance of his personage as an historical figure worthy of respect, if not admiration and perhaps even love.

Certainly, his ethical and moral teachings should be considered in the same light as the world views of other renowned philosophical and spiritual leaders. These would include the great Greek and Roman Philosophers, Confucius, Siddhartha Gautama (Buddha), and others closer to us in time such as Mahatma Gandhi, Dr. Martin Luther King Jr. and the Dali Lama.

Author's Remarks

The writing of this book has been a wonderful journey for me and has led me to a deeper appreciation of the positive influence Jesus has had upon humanity, above and beyond the Christian community. As the occasion arose, I entered words of wisdom (hopefully) and anecdotes that came to me as I was writing about a particular biblical passage. I hope they did not detract from the main purpose of the book. While engaged in entering these sidebars, I had to resist the desire to enter others, since the book was written to amplify Jesus teachings, rather than as a forum for my collection of aphorisms. However, there are a few that were not entered earlier that the reader may find of interest; they follow:

On Forgiveness and Redemption

There are many examples of Jesus' belief in humanity's ability to redeem itself for transgressions in the Gospels; certainly, the "Prodigal Son" (Luke 15:11-32, See Page 54) is one of the most inspiring examples. There are many more examples of this; one of the most striking that I recall occurred in the Academy Award winning movie "Gandhi." The scene occurs during a period of widespread violence between Hindus and Muslims, following India's freedom from British rule. Gandhi (played by Ben Kingsley) has gone on a long hunger strike to stop the violence, which comes to a climax as a group of Hindus and Muslims come to tell him that the rioting has stopped. Just as the men are departing, one rushes back, and with blazing eyes tells Gandhi that he is going to Hell because he killed a Muslim child, declaring "I crushed his head against a wall." Gandhi tells the despondent man that "there is a way out of Hell;" he tells the man that he must find an orphan child and raise him as his own – but adds, "the child must be Muslim and you must raise him as one."

On Leading a Virtuous Life

Another story, which came to me while contemplating the aphorisms I included at the end of "The Conditions of Discipleship" (See Page 103), is ascribed to the Native American Cherokee Nation. Paraphrasing: "When you were born, you cried and the world rejoiced. Live your life so that when you die, the world cries and you rejoice." Interestingly, Christians are taught to "rejoice" when dying in the belief that they will be "reborn" into eternal life.

On Ignorance and Prejudice

Another striking story came to me when contemplating Mark 8:18-21 and what I had written about Charles Dickens' *A Christmas Carol.* Dickens' classic is arguably one of the most inspiring books ever written about redemption, whose retelling has been the subject of countless movie, television and live productions, and a holiday "must see" for many. There is a vivid scene in the acclaimed 1953 version of the movie that occurs as the Ghost of Christmas Present is about to depart from Scrooge (played by Alistair Sim). Opening his robes, the spirit reveals two ragged children. Upon seeing their dreadful state, Scrooge asks the ghost if the children were his. The ghost answers: "They are Man's . . . they cling to me for protection from their fetters . . . [121] This boy is Ignorance. This girl is Want. Beware them both . . . but most of all beware this boy."

In the movie, the ghost offers no explanation for this warning. However, the words are amplified in the novel; the scene occurs at the end of Stave Three. Thereunder Dickens' writes that the word "DOOM" could be seen upon the boy's brow. Since Dickens' tale was clearly written as a moral indictment of the society he lived in, it appears that he believed that "ignorance" was the most dangerous of all man's faults. It is hard to argue with that warning or with the fact that ignorance, and its handmaiden prejudice, have only prospered since Dickens inked those words more than 170 years ago.

On Things That Inspire Us

While contemplating the electric effect Jesus must have had upon those who witnessed his "Sermon on the Mount" (Matthew 7:28-29 – See Page 87.), I thought of how a non-Christian like Mahatma Gandhi was so inspired by it that he recited part of it in his morning prayers, nearly two thousand years later. While doing so it came to me that the closest I could come to that in my own experience would be when I saw my wife giving birth to my sons, or the first time I saw the Lincoln Memorial, or heard Martin Luther King's "I Have a Dream" speech.

A more recent, albeit a bit less dramatic experience, occurred as I watched a scene from the critically acclaimed movie, *The Shawshank Redemption*. If you are a fan of the movie, you will recall a truly memorable scene wherein Andy Dufrense (played by Tim Robbins) plays an opera piece over the prison's loudspeaker system, transporting the entire prison population (and the moviegoers) to a place of momentary reverie, as "those two Italian ladies" (spoken by "Red," played by Morgan Freeman) began singing a beautiful aria.[122]

Another memorable example can be seen (and heard) in Luciano Pavarotti's 1994 live performance of Puccini's "*Nessun*

Dorma" (No one is sleeping). *YouTube* has a version, but the quality of sound is not great. Indeed, Jesus' persona must have been truly inspiring given all those who carried on so tirelessly after he was no longer with them.

On the Love of Children

One last inspiring story I'd like to share came to me while contemplating Jesus' love of children and his message in Luke 12:34 (See Page 122), wherein Jesus tells his disciples:

> *"For where your treasure is, there also will your heart be."*

I once read that we can learn what others truly love by the amount of time they devote to a particular thing. If we see a man washing and polishing his car frequently, we know he does this because he loves his car. Children sense this, which is the reason some authorities believe that the most important thing we can do for our children is simply to spend time *with* them. I think this fosters the most precious gift parents can give a child, the belief that they are worthy of being loved.

There is a theory that, child prodigies aside, it takes ten thousand hours of concentrated practice to become truly accomplished in fields such as music and chess. Would that we spend even a fraction of this amount of time perfecting the art of parenting.

* * *

Final Comments

As it was for me, I hope the contemplation of Jesus' teachings and the Gospel passages entered above led the readers to discover context within their own life experiences, as well as parallels to inspirational messages they have come across. I also found myself asking a lot of questions and wanting to explore details, such as what coin might the Gospels have been referring to in the "Render unto Caesar" passage (the denarius; see Page 52) and what was the size of a mustard seed (See Page 96), and so on. Trusting that the reader might find the answers of interest as well, I included the results of some of my own studies into these details throughout the book.

Perhaps the readers likewise tallied their own thoughts and comments as they went along and would like a forum to express them. Should this interest exist in readers in some number, I will endeavor to find an appropriate way to address them, perhaps through an interactive website. Please feel free to send me any stories, comments, or criticisms you may have to *oscar@northstreampublishing.com* .

Credits

Books and Publications

Alcoholics Anonymous (the Big Book). A. A. World Wide Services, Inc., 1955. Print.

Benis, Jonathan. *A Rabbi Looks at Jesus of Nazareth.* Chosen Books, 2011. Print

Campbell, Joseph. *The Hero With A Thousand Faces.* New World Library (Third Edition), 2008. Print

Dockery, K., Goodwin, J. & P. *The Student Bible Dictionary.* Barbour, 2000. Print

Grant, Michael. *Jesus – An Historians Review of the Gospels.* C. Scribner's Sons, 1971. Print.

Hahn, Thich Nhat. *Going Home – Jesus and Buddha as Brothers.* Riverhead Books, 1999. Print

Hart, Roy Hanu, *Faith in a Hurting World.* Info Faith Communications, Inc, 2009. Print

Hays, Gregory. *Marcus Aurelius – Meditations.* Random House, Inc., 2002. Print

His Holiness The Dalai Lama. The Good Heart – A Buddhist Perspective on the Teachings of Jesus. Wisdom Publications, 1996. Print

Hudson, Christopher, D. *How Jesus Changed the World.* Barbour, 2016. Print.

Miller, Stephan, M. *The Complete Guide To The Bible.* Barbour, 2007. Print

National Geographic. *The Story of Jesus.* Time Life Books, 2016. Print.

O'Reilly, Bill and Dugard, Martin. *Killing Jesus.* Henry Holt & Co. NY, 2013. Print.

Satprakashananda, Swami. *Hinduism and Christianity – Jesus Christ and His Teachings in light of the Vedanta*. Vedanta Press, 1975. Print

Schwortz, Barrie, M. *The Shroud of Turin Changed my Life.* Readers Digest, Mar. 2010. Article

Strobel, Lee. The *Case For Christ.* Zondervan, Grand Rapids, MI, 1998. Print.

United States Conference of Catholic Bishops, Washington, D.C. *New American Bible, Revised Edition*, copyright 2010, 1991, 1986, 1970, Confraternity of Christian Doctrine, Inc., Washington, D.C. Print

Wilson, Ian. *Jesus: The Evidence*. Harper & Row Publishers, Inc., 1984. Print.

Websites

Encyclopedia Britannica, (*http://www.britannica.com*)

Judaism 101, (*http://www.jewfaq.org*)

New Advent, The Catholic Encyclopedia (*http://www.newadvent.org/cathen/*)

Shroud of Turin, (*http://www.shroud.com*)

United States Conference of Catholic Bishops, (*http://www. usccb.com*)

Wikipedia, (http://www.wikipedia.org)

Acknowledgments

It is customary and altogether appropriate for an author to give thanks to those who helped in the writing and publishing of their work. Aside from those touched on in the Foreword, I also wish to thank my children, family, and friends, and partner Mary Martin, for their encouragement and support. I also wish to thank John Clifton of Foley Square Books, New York, NY for his thoughtful assistance in designing and formatting the book as well as assisting in its publication. A special thank-you to Nadine Moroch Schneider of South Mountain Studio, LLC, New City, NY, who helped edit the book and acted as design consultant. Their patient, skilled, and experienced assistance and encouragement were invaluable to this first-time author.

Index

Notes

[1] M. K. Gandhi, *"Discussion with a Missionary,"* 65:79–82. Collected Works of Mahatma Gandhi, April 14, 1937. Print

[2] The *Pharisees* were a group of self-appointed protectors of Jewish law, which encompassed both civil and spiritual matters, and were recognized as experts in both. Some Pharisees were also *Scribes*, who were officials with the authority to prepare contracts, including those for marriage and divorce, and legal documents for the sale of land, mortgages, loans, etc. Every village had a Scribe. The *Sadducees* were a party of high priests, aristocratic families, and wealthy merchants who maintained the Great Temple in Jerusalem (See note 4). The Sadducees had other roles as well, including as leaders in the religious, social, and political functions of the church.

[3] Stoning is the world's oldest form of capital punishment, prescribed for various defined offenses in religious and civil codes dating back as far as the beginning of recorded history. The practice, still carried on today in the Middle East, can involve burying the condemned up the waist for men, or the shoulders for women, after which they are pelted with stones by a crowd of volunteers until death was assured. The stones were carefully chosen for size so that no one blow could cause death, to both prolong the suffering, which could last for more than twenty minutes, and to ensure that no one person would be accountable for the death, much like today's firing squad. The practice was extremely painful, gruesome, and degrading, with the condemned suffering multiple contusions, welts, broken bones, and profuse bleeding about the head; often leaving the individual unrecognizable, even to his or her own family.

[4] Interestingly, the Sadducees were in constant conflict with the more liberal Pharisees on matters of religious interpretation, as they refused to accept anything beyond the Torah (the first five books of the Old Testament, written by Moses), while the Pharisees accepted the oral traditions that had been added to the Torah. The Gospels tell us that some of the Pharisees even sought out Jesus to discuss his interpretations of Jewish law.

[5] While Jesus is traditionally depicted as a carpenter, the term recorded in the Gospels was translated into English from the Greek word *tekton*, which means "craftsman." In the village where Jesus grew up, a craftsman could have been a carpenter or a stonemason, which were equally respected trades.

[6] Khalil Gibran, *The Prophet*, Knopf, New York, 1911, Page 29. Print

[7] G. K. Chesterton may have expressed it best: "The Christian ideal has not been tried and found wanting; it has been found difficult and left untried." *What's Wrong with the World*. Dodd, Mead, New York 1910

[8] Jesus referred to himself as the *Son of Man* numerous times in the Gospels, as in Matthew 8:18-20, Page 89 (also, Mark 2:10, 9:9; Matthew 24:27, etc.) His use of the term is no doubt taken from the Old Testament, wherein the address was used many times to denote man's lowly status compared with God, and perhaps as a reminder that all men are descendants of the first man, Adam.

[9] There were originally twelve Apostles (from the Greek "delegate"), the number may have been inspired by the twelve tribes of Israel. The Apostles included Simon called Peter (from the Greek word for "rock"); Andrew, Peter's brother; James and John, the sons of Zebedee, who were fishing partners of Peter; Philip; Bartholomew; Thomas (also called Didymus); Matthew, the tax collector; James, the son of Alphaeus; Thaddeus; Simon the Cananean (called the Zealot); and Judas Iscariot. The Gospels tell us that Judas would later betray Jesus and hang himself in remorse. Tradition holds that ten of the remaining Apostles were martyred, save for John, who, though immersed in boiling oil to silence him, survived.

[10] From the Greek word *euangelion*, meaning "good news" or "message"

[11] Based on the author's review of John 8.7 and other analogous passages this seemingly senseless act may have been done to distract the Church officials and the crowd that accompanied them from their intended purpose, and blunt their immediate passion. Jesus' simple action may have been a sophisticated device that he would use time and again in his short ministry, as evidenced in the Gospel passages that followed. (Mt. 22: 15, Page 52).

[12] The name Jesus comes from translations of the Aramaic name "Yeshua." In the time of Jesus, last names were taken from the town where the person was born, or taken from the father's name. Jesus would have simply been called "Jesus of Nazareth," or "Jesus, son of Joseph". Since early Christian times Jesus' followers added the word "Christ" to his name, from the Greek *Christos*, or "the anointed one," as the early Greeks had no equivalent for the Aramaic word *Masiah*, which is now translated as "Messiah" in English

[13] Hinduism, which traces its beginnings to 3,000 BC, is not as much a religious practice as it is a way of life. The most traditional school of Hindu teachings follow the Sanatana Dharna, which defines an

eternal order of duties all Hindu's must follow, as delineated above. Like the followers of Jesus, most Hindus believe in a Supreme being and the eternal soul, or Atman. Interestingly, Hindus see a parallel between Jesus and Krishna (a major Deity), who is a God of compassion, tenderness and love. Tradition holds that both had a virgin mother (Mary was visited by the holy spirit, Devaki by Vishnu): both were saved by a spirit messenger from ruler who sought to slay him; both visited by shepherds: both are credited with many miracles, and both were resurrected from the dead. In addition, both Hindu priests, monks and nuns and Jesus' disciples and Catholic Clergy are called to lead a monastic life and the celibacy. I was also surprised to learn that there are Mother Mary temples and shrines throughout India, where millions venerate Jesus' mother Mary as the Blessed Virgin.

[14] Mahatma Gandhi, the great Hindu leader who led the non-violent, non-cooperative movement that freed India from 200 years of British rule, was a great admirer of Jesus. In fact, his morning and evening prayer rituals consisted of reading passages from both the Bhagavad Gita and the Sermon on the Mount. Gandhi said he believed "Jesus was one of mankind's greatest teachers" and a "transcendental figure for **all** (emphasis supplied) mankind."

[15] Buddhism principles can be summed up in the Four Noble Truths which state that life is suffering; suffering is primarily the result of unsatisfied desires and hate; happiness and contentment can only be achieved if we surrender our ego and self-centeredness; and we must continue to follow the path of the Noble Truth's to find wisdom, and if we practice these truths in all our thoughts and actions and develop compassion for others, we may reach true enlightenment, and end the cycle of death and rebirth. One can find a great deal of similarity between the Noble Truth's and Jesus teachings, particularly in the Sermon on the Mount wherein Jesus' words echo the Nobel Truths, that life is suffering, as Jesus speaks of the poor in spirit, the meek, those who are persecuted, and those who mourn and those who hunger for justice (taken from the Beatitudes). Jesus spoke to the second Noble Truth in many ways as well, telling his followers that they must surrender their egos and desires for earthly pleasures. However, while Jesus tells his followers that the way to end suffering is to follow his teachings and that the end of the suffering, if one lives a life of virtue, will be heaven. Buddhists believe the living a life of virtue will lead to Nirvana; but it is a solitary journey, with Buddha's teachings lighting the way. Other practices that are similar include a monastic lifestyle (Catholic and Buddhist priests, monks and nuns are celibate) and that meditation and prayer are important

to both faiths. Like Hindus, both observe rites of worship, physical symbols and adornments in their buildings, and other respects, as well.

[16] The passage was taken from the Sermon on the Mount (Matthew Chapter 5 Verses 38 to 42). Interestingly, this is the very same passage that Mahatma Gandhi, a Hindu, referred to when asked about his non-violent, non-cooperative movement that freed India from British rule.

[17] Throughout his ministry, Jesus told his followers to be faithful to what Christians call the Old Testament, and the Gospels contain numerous accounts where Jesus employed passages from the Old Testament to reinforce his message. In Matthew 5:17-19 Jesus tells his followers *"Do not think that I have come to abolish the law of the prophets. I have come not to abolish but to fulfill . . . whoever breaks one of the least of these commandments and teaches others to do so will be called least in the kingdom of heaven."*

[18] Mohammad was born in 570AD and died at the age of 62. Islam is the world's second-largest religion after Christianity with 1.8 B followers. Muslims believe the word of God was revealed many times through Mohammad and other prophets including Adam, Abraham, Moses and Jesus. Muslims believe that their holy book, the Quran is the final and inviolate word of God.

[19] Most notably the writings of Tacitus, a first-century Roman historian and senator, and Pliny the Younger, a Roman magistrate who condemned early Christians to death. Other compelling historical documents were written by the Greek Historian Thallus, which some scholars believe include a reference to Jesus that dates to within twenty years of his crucifixion, based on Thallus's description of a darkness that fell over the earth and earthquakes. Another noted historian of the period, Josephus, although born a Jew, became a member of the imperial household in Rome, where he wrote several books on Jewish history, including an autobiography, *Antiquities of the Jews*, which mentions both Jesus and John the Baptist.

[20] Traditionally, the term "AD" or "A.D." is placed before the year to signify events which occurred after Jesus was born and "BC" or "B.C." is used to date events prior to the birth of Jesus. The terms CE or C.E. ("Common Era") and BCE or B.C.E. have come into vogue as the non-Christian equivalents of AD and BC. The terms AD and BC will be employed in this writing for continuity.

[21] Christians regard the four Gospels of Matthew, Mark, Luke, and

John as the authoritative scripture of the New Testament, which cannot be added to, changed, or deleted. These Gospels are the "Canon" (from the Greek word for "rule") for all Christianity.

[22] The "Criterion of Embarrassment" holds that anyone fabricating a document would *not* have invented historical accounts that would embarrass and weaken its message, such as seen in the crucifixion of Jesus, as this method of execution was considered the most shameful and degrading in the Roman Empire, which is where Jesus' disciples intended to seek converts. (Interestingly, Muslims believe that Jesus, who is revered as a great prophet in the Qur'an, was not crucified but, like Muhammad, was raised directly to heaven in Jerusalem by Allah, which is Aramaic for "God") There are many other examples of this criterion in the Gospels, such as the passages concerning Jesus' interaction with women, which was forbidden at that time, and particularly Jesus' words during what has become known as the "Last Supper" (Page 149, Matthew 26:26-30). The Gospels also contain many passages of Jesus' confrontations with the Jewish religious leaders of that time, virtually all of whom were denounced by Jesus as hypocrites. Since Jesus sought the acceptance of his teachings by his fellow Jews, the alienation of their civil and religious leaders would seem to be counterintuitive, as well.

[23] The term "Old Testament" is used by Christians to refer to the traditional Jewish Scriptures, the last of which predates the life of Jesus by more than four hundred years. Catholic bibles include fifty books from the Old Testament, from the Pentateuch, or first five books of the Jewish Bible (Genesis, Exodus, Leviticus, Numbers, and Deuteronomy), through Malachi. The term "New Testament" was given to the Christian Scriptures, as Christians believe that Jesus fulfilled the promise of the Old Testament.

[24] Christianity, in its various practices, accounts for about one-third of the world's peoples, followed by Islam, which is the faith of about 21 percent of the world's people.

[25] While this writing will focus on Jesus' teachings with limited reference to the miracles that have been ascribed to him, there is no doubt that the Apostles were inspired by something beyond his words, and no discourse on the impact Jesus has had upon the world would be complete without a discussion on what may be the most cogent explanation of Jesus' rise from obscurity to the world's most recognized figure.

[26] Saint Augustine is considered one of the Roman Catholic Church's greatest theologians, and the Roman Church has accepted

his teaching about free will. Saint Augustine wrote that while God knows who will be saved and who will not, with no possibility that one destined to be lost will be saved, this knowledge represents God's perfect knowledge of how humans will freely choose their destinies. Thus, while the moral roads each of us take are of our own choosing, God knows where they will end.

[27] Although Galileo was originally tried for heresy by the Roman Catholic Church for his heliocentric theory (the Sun, not the Earth, is the center of our solar system), he remained a devout Catholic throughout his life; in fact, his two daughters were nuns. Additionally, it may be noted that although Galileo himself did not consider his writings about heliocentricity to be heretical (while Galileo believed that the Bible could not err, any assumed difference between it and the natural sciences was the result of interpretation) his Catholic leaders at that time did. Today the Catholic Church does not consider heliocentricity or any of Galileo's writings to be heretical. (Rich Deem, "*Famous Scientists Who Believed in God*," last modified 19 May 2005, on "*Evidence for God from Science*" website. *http://www.godandscience.org/apologetics/sciencefaith.html)*

[28] Mahatma Gandhi. who was a great admirer of Jesus (he even had an image of Jesus in his house) and well versed in the Gospels, once said on the subject: "I am sure that if he were living here now among men, he would bless the lives of many who perhaps have never even heard his name, if only their lives embodied the virtues of which he was a living example on earth; the virtues of loving one's neighbor as oneself and of doing good and charitable works among one's fellowmen." (Prabhu, R.K. *What Jesus Means to Me*. N.p.: n.p., 1959. N. Page. Print.

[29] Excerpted from a 1962 statement King made in response to criticism from some Christian supporters who were disturbed when he agreed to serve as honorary chairman of the Gandhi Society.

[30] The author included passages from the current Roman Catholic (RC) Gospels as published in the *New American Bible, Revised Edition*, copyright 2010, 1991, 1986, 1970, Confraternity of Christian Doctrine, Inc., Washington, D.C. United States Conference of Catholic Bishops, Washington, D.C., Publisher. ISBN 978-1-60137-486-8. This was done for purposes of uniformity. While there are differences in the wording in and among the various Christian Gospels, such as between the KJV, (whose verses may be more familiar to the reader) and the accepted Catholic translations from the Greek, that is not viewed as significant, since Jesus' message is clearly contained in all major Christian Bibles. Should readers desire to read cited verses of

the Gospels more fully, from the RC translation or from another Christian source, they are invited to do so.

[31] Some scriptural scholars and theologians have written that the reference was made in connections with Jesus' nieces, nephews, and cousins – as the Semitic language made no distinction – and passages in the Old Testament (such as in Gn 14:16, Gn 29:15, Lv 10:4, Dt 23:8 and Neh. 5:7) employ the same term in circumstances, and the reference there is clearly made about a cousin, rather than a brother.

[32] *The disciples approached him and said, "Why do you speak to them in parables?" He said to them in reply, "Because knowledge of the mysteries of the kingdom of heaven has been granted to you, but to them it has not been granted. (Matthew 13:10-11)*

[33] Jesus used the example of the mustard seed to admonish his disciples for their lack of faith. See Matthew 17:20. Page 104.

[34] In 1958 Pope John XXIII called for a worldwide council, later to be known as Vatican II, to address the relationship of the Roman Catholic Church to the modern world. The result was a far-reaching refinement of Church dogma, including that with respect to the Church's teachings concerning other faiths. One of the principal documents to ensue from the council was the "*Lumen Gentium*" (Latin for "Light of the Nations"), which included the following, excerpted from paragraph 16: "For it is He who gives to all men life and breath and all things, and as Savior wills that *all men* [emphasis added] be saved. . . . Nor does Divine Providence deny the helps necessary for salvation to those who, without blame on their part, have not yet arrived at an explicit knowledge of God and with His grace strive to live a good life."

[35] The Gospels contain extensive passages identifying women as individuals, many by name. Aside from Jesus' mother Mary, others whose names are prominently noted in the Gospels include Mary's cousin Martha, as well as Elizabeth, the mother of John the Baptist and Mary Magdalene, a follower of some note, who stood at the cross while Jesus was crucified, while his Apostles hid in terror. The Gospels also include the names of Mary and Martha, the sisters of Jesus' beloved friend Lazarus, and Joanna, the wife of King Herod's household manager, and others.

[36] The Introduction of this book and John 8:7 (Page 50) record Jesus' refusal to condemn a woman, at the risk of his own life. See also later discussions in Matthew 5:27-32, Page 68 and Matthew 25:1-13, Page 146.

[37] Samaritans, who numbered more than one million, were adherents of an Abrahamic religion (descendants of Abraham, which included Jews, Christians, and Muslims) were considered heretics by Jews of that time because they refused to accept all the practices of the Jewish nation upon its return from Babylon, where it had been exiled by the Assyrians. Samaritans were treated with contempt by the Jews, and were not allowed to sacrifice in the Great Temple in Jerusalem, nor were marriages between Jews and Samarians considered legal.

[38] *"Do not think that I have come to bring peace upon the earth. I have come to bring not peace but the sword. For I have come to set a man against his father, a daughter against her mother, and a daughter-in-law against her mother-in-law"* (Matthew 10:34-35).

[39] While certain religious groups consider some of these practices valid, the Roman Catholic Church and other orthodox faiths condemn the use of abortion (except where the life of the mother is at stake), and believe that marriage between couples of the same sex is not sanctified by God.

[40] In April 2016 Pope Francis I released a lengthy Apostolic Exhortation or Papal Bull entitled Amoris Laetitia, which is Latin for "The Joy of Love". The letter contained the Pope's instructions to the faithful on many social and religious practices and included the following words, "We would like before all else to reaffirm that every person, regardless of sexual orientation, ought to be respected in his or her dignity and treated with consideration, while 'every sign of unjust discrimination' is to be carefully avoided, particularly any form of aggression and violence."

[41] The term "Render unto Caesar" (KJV Matthew 22:21) is used here as it is undoubtedly the most familiar to the reader. The RC version reads *"Then repay to Caesar what belongs to Caesar and to God what belongs to God."* (Matthew 22:15)

[42] The commonly used term comes from a tenth-century Christian abbé, Saint Bernard of Clairvaux.

[43] The term "white lie" dates back to the 16th century, along with its companion "black lie." The white lie is about a small or unimportant matter that someone tells to avoid hurting another person, whereas the black lie's intent is to purposely hurt someone.

[44] In all fairness, while Jesus held the Church officials in contempt for what he saw as an abuse of their power and a failure to faithfully follow God's laws, they clearly believed that Jesus was a false prophet and not the Messiah whose coming was foretold in the Old

Testament. Since this writing is not intended to persuade the reader of the divinity of Jesus but simply to illuminate the wisdom of his words, the subject need not be broached. Thankfully, after thousands of years of open hostility and unjust persecution of Jews by Christians, many modern Christians and Jews look more to their common morality than to their differences. We are all familiar with the term "Judeo-Christian tradition," and the world is a much better place for this reconciliation.

[45] The coin produced would have been a denarius, which was the value of one day's wage for a common laborer or soldier. The denarius of that day had the head of the Roman emperor Tiberius on one side, and on the other side a likeness of his mother, Livia, shown holding an olive branch and a scepter, personifying imperial Rome. Since the Jews were required to convert all of their foreign coinage to shekels in the Temple, Jesus' request for the Roman denarius resulted in the gathered crowd searching for one; there again distracting and blunting the passion of those who were seeking his destruction.

[46] While Jesus' response may seem uninspired, his answer was perfect, for it dampened the crowd's immediate passion, since no one had the Roman coin used to pay the census tax. (Only Shekels could be brought into the Temple.) So the church elders had to send for one. And producing it was an admission that the church elders themselves were paying the tax and could not very well claim that doing so was a violation of Jewish law.

[47] Jefferson penned these now famous lines in a January 1, 1802 letter written in reply to one sent him by a Danbury Connecticut church. In that letter, Jefferson intoned: "I contemplate with sovereign reverence that act of the whole American people which declared that their legislature should 'make no law respecting an establishment of religion, or prohibiting the free exercise thereof,' thus building a wall of separation between Church and State."

[48] Pope, Alexander. *An Essay on Criticism*, Part 2. N.p.: n.p.1711. Print

[49] Tolstoy, Leo. *Where Love Is, There Is God Also*,. N.p.: n.d. Print.

[50] In the Old Testament, "righteous" referred to those who conduct themselves in accordance with God's will. Today it has come to mean one who is virtuous, generous, fair, and just.

[51] The Gospel of Mark is viewed as having been written before AD 70.

[52] Many Orthodox Christians celebrate Christmas on January 7,

based on the Gregorian Calendar, which is December 25 in the Julian Calendar.

[53] Many early cultures celebrated rituals around December 25, including the Northern European feast of Yuletide. The Romans celebrated Saturnalia around this time, as well, and Druidic and pagans celebrated the winter solstice. Biblical historians now believe that Jesus was born in March, since the Gospels' description of Jesus' birth make mention of shepherds watching over the newly born lambs, which would have occurred in the spring.

[54] Early Christians used the symbol of a fish () to identify one another to avoid detection and the persecution that was sure to follow if they were discovered. While some believe that the symbol was chosen from the Greek word for fish, *ichthus*, as the Greek letters of the word form an anagram for the phrase "Jesus Christ, Son of God, Savior," others see its roots in the calling of Jesus to his first Apostles, who were fishermen. Interestingly, the hand signal that early Christians used to identify each other represented a fish, and was given as crossed fingers, which have come down to us as a gesture for good luck ("keep your fingers crossed") and when held behind the back as a means of seeking silent pardon (especially among children) for fibbing.

[55] "But the New Testament produced a different impression, especially the Sermon on the Mount which went straight to my heart. I compared it with the Gita. The verses, 'But I say unto you, that ye resist not evil: but whosoever shall smite thee on thy right cheek, turn to him the other also. And if any man take away thy coat let him have thy cloak too,' delighted me beyond measure and put me in mind of Shamal Bhatt's 'For a bowl of water, give a goodly meal'. (Bhatt, Shamal, *For a Bowl of Water, Give a Goodly Meal*, N.p. : n.p., 1958. Print.)

[56] Dr. King was a great admirer of Gandhi and once said, "Christ gave us the goals and Mahatma Gandhi the tactics." (Tougas, Shelly. Birmingham 1963: *How a Photograph Rallied Civil Rights Support*, Mankto, MN: Compass Point, 2011. Print.)

[57] The Mosaic law includes the Ten Commandments that God gave to the Israelites through Moses, as well as many rules of religious observance given in the first five books of the Old Testament, which in Judaism is called the Torah.

[58] Mark 10:12 concludes this passage with the words "*and if she divorces her husband and marries another, she commits adultery.*"

[59] Luke 6:36 uses the word "*merciful*".

[60] Laura Hillenbrand, author of the best-seller *Sea Biscuit*, wrote of his experiences in *Unbroken: A World War II Story of Survival, Resilience, and Redemption*. The book was later adapted into a motion picture film directed by Angelina Jolie, *Unbroken*, starring Jack O'Connell as Zamperini.

[61] From a series of lectures delivered on the Canadian Broadcasting Corporation in late 1967; later published following his assassination. King, Martin Luther. *The Trumpet of Conscience*. New York: Harper & Row, 1968. Print.

[62] In Mt. 5, as noted earlier, Jesus enjoins us to pray for our enemies; in Mt. 9 he tells us to pray for vocations; in Mt. 24 he urges us to pray to be relieved of temptation. In Lk. 18 Jesus gives us a parable about a widow and a judge who had rendered an unfair judgment, but through her persistence she finally receives justice. Jesus tells us to pray to the Father in the same way as we do when we give to charity, that is, inconspicuously.

[63] Leo F. Buscaglia. *The way of the Bull*, Page 6. Charles B. Slack, Inc., Thorofare, NJ, 1973. Print.

[64] Gandhi, Mohandas Karamchand. Young India, weekly publication 23-1, 1930.

[65] Step 2 of Alcoholics Anonymous reads: "Came to believe that a power greater than ourselves could restore us to sanity." As a relevant aside, virtually everyone who has attended a 12-step program meeting knows the "Serenity Prayer". Few however know it was written by American theologian and minister Karl Paul Reinhold Niebuhr. The original text reads "Father, give us courage to change what must be altered, serenity to accept what cannot be helped, and the insight to know the one from the other."

[66] The prayer entered above is the one most familiar to Christians and differs a bit from the wording in Matthew. Mark gives the last line as "*deliver us from the evil one.*" (emphasis added)

[67] The term "Sufficient unto the Day" (KJV) may be more familiar to the reader. It is an aphorism for the viewpoint that one should live in the present.

[68] Leo F. Buscaglia. *The Way of the Bull*. Charles B. Slack, Inc., Thorofare, NJ, 1973. Print.

[69] For an explanation of "scribe," see Note 2

[70] While Jesus' disciples referred to him as the *"Son of God"* throughout the Gospels, he referred to himself as the *"Son of Man."* This occurs for the first time Mark 2:10 and in Matthew Chapter 8. This was discussed earlier in the footnotes in the Foreword of this book.

[71] The historian Flavius Josephus (AD 37–100) recorded a narrative of John the Baptist's missionary life and death at the hands of Herod Antipas.

[72] Jews and Christians celebrate the Sabbath on different days. In the book of Genesis, God made the heavens and earth in six days and rested on the seventh. Since Sunday is traditionally the first day, the seventh day would be Saturday, which is the day Jews attend service. Christians, on the other hand, attend service on the eighth "Lord's Day," Sunday, as that is the day they believe Jesus arose from the dead and fulfilled the promise of the Old Testament, thus completing creation.

[73] "A house divided against itself cannot stand. I believe this government cannot endure permanently half-slave and half-free. I do not expect the Union to be dissolved—I do not expect the house to fall—but I do expect it will cease to be divided. It will become all one thing or all the other."

[74] Schroeder, Gerald *"Your Life, Your Judaism."* N.p.: n.p. pag. Print

[75] The word "Passover" comes from the Old Testament's account of the Jews being led by Moses out of bondage in Egypt, as recorded in the book of Exodus. The term refers to the last of ten plagues God wrought on Egypt, causing the death of all their firstborn sons. The Jews were instructed to mark their doorposts with the blood of the newly killed spring lambs so that the angel of death would "pass over" those dwellings. While the term "Passover" has come into common use, Jews use the term *Pesakh*, which commemorates the seven or eight-day celebration of their freedom from bondage. The celebration commences at sundown with a Seder meal in which the story of their liberation from Egypt is retold.

[76] Jewish tradition handed down by Moses allowed a man to divorce his wife by simply handing her a bill of divorce (Dt. 24:1); therefore, the Pharisees believed that Jesus' teaching on the matter was heretical.

[77] Jesus also declared that divorce is permitted if the marriage is "unlawful" the meaning of which is discussed above (Page 69).

[78] Jesus' words here were obviously intended to dissuade all but the

most fervent believers in his message from attempting to become one of his disciples; indeed, some of Jesus' good friends were wealthy, including Joseph of Arimathea and Zacchaerius. Moreover, Christian theology does not demand that its adherents give *everything* they own to the poor. Obviously, if they did that there would soon be nothing left to give, and they too would join the ranks of the needy. Instead, Christians and Jews are called upon to "tithe," that is, to give one-tenth of their earnings to charity. Muslims as well are called to give alms in proportion to wealth.

[79] The road referred to in Luke ran from Jerusalem to Jericho and existed in the time of Jesus. It was known as the "Way of Blood" because "of the blood which is often shed there by robbers." Wilkinson, *The Way from Jerusalem to Jericho,* The Biblical Archaeologist, Vol 38, No. 1 (Mar., 1975) pp. 10-14

[80] Samaritans were a group of neighboring people despised by Jews, as entered above at Page 42 – "The Woman of Samaria" (John. 4:1-42).

[81] Mahatma Gandhi's "Seven Social Sins" were "Wealth without work, Pleasure without conscience, Knowledge without character, Commerce without morality, Science without humanity, Worship without sacrifice, and Politics without principle." Mohandas Karamchand Gandhi, *Young India*, October 22, 1925.

[82] Rowling, J.K. *Harry Potter and the Deathly Hallows*, Page 325. Scholastic, Inc., New York, 2007. Print.

[83] Rowling, J. K. *Harry Potter and the Deathly Hallows*, Page 328. Scholastic, Inc., New York, 2007. Print

[84] As noted in the opening section of this work, "Does Jesus Condemn Non-Christians?" (Page 38), Jesus' words here have meaning to Christians and non-Christians alike.

[85] Per the "Introduction" to the Gospel According to John, United States Conference of Catholic Bishops, Washington, D.C. *New American Bible, Revised.*

[86] Nicodemus has been accorded sainthood by the Roman Catholic Church and the Eastern Orthodox and Byzantine Catholics. Tradition has it that Nicodemus was martyred sometime in the first century of the Christian era.

[87] Manna was the bread the Jews received from heaven after being led from bondage by Moses.

[88] Matthew 26:26-30 (Page 150)

[89] The temple known as the "Great Temple" was located in Jerusalem and remains the holiest site in Judaism, as it is believed to be a place where God's presence was revealed more than anywhere else. Besides being the holiest city on earth to Christians and Jews, it is also an important religious site to Muslims, who believe that the Prophet Muhammad (as well as Jesus) was raised to heaven in Jerusalem. The first "Temple" was built by King Solomon and completed in 957 BC. Following its first destruction by the Babylonians in 586 BC, it was rebuilt in 516 BC (Ezr. 5) by the Persian king Darius the Great. The Temple was substantially rebuilt and greatly expanded in 20–18 BC by Herod the Great, who died a few years before Jesus was born. Herod's expansion included the Temple Mount, which encompassed the Great Temple, and the construction of a surrounding plaza, said to have been the 36 acres in size, which allowed for the accommodation of the huge crowds that came on pilgrimages and festivals, including Passover. The Temple and the city of Jerusalem were destroyed by the Romans in AD 70, following a Jewish revolt. Only the lower levels of the Western Wall (known today as the "Wailing Wall") remain from the original site.

[90] Lent, from the Old English words *Len-ten*, or spring season, refers to the traditional forty-day period (actually 46 days, counting Sundays) commencing on Ash Wednesday, and culminating on Easter Sunday. Lent is a solemn period of prayer, fasting, and reflection observed by many Christian denominations, including the Roman Catholic, Eastern Orthodox, Anglican, Lutheran and Methodist churches. The forty-days commemorate the time Jesus spent fasting in the desert before he began his public ministry.(See Page 61)

[91] For example, John Chapter 12 records Jesus stopping in Bethany the day before he entered Jerusalem, while Matthew Chapter 26 records the event occurring a day after Jesus' entry into Jerusalem.

[92] The word "Hosanna" comes from the Hebrew words meaning "O Lord grant salvation." The passage is part of a song sung at Passover as entered in the Psalm 118:26 of the Old Testament. Christians include readings from the Old Testament, including the singing of Psalms, as part of their service liturgies.

[93] Genesis 3:19

[94] Jews were required to pay for the services of the Temple priests in shekels and so had to change any Roman or Greek coinage they had with the Temple money changers. While animals to be used in sacrifice were generally penned outside the Temple Mount, the Chief Priests allowed some merchants to keep them in the Temple area.

[95] Drysdale, William *"Proverbs From Plymouth Pulpit"*; Selected From the Writings And Sayings of Henry Ward Beecher; D. Appleton and Company, NY, Publisher 1887. Print.

[96] The Mount of Olives (Mount Olivet) is a mountain near Jerusalem's Old City, and is named for the olive groves that once covered its slopes. The Gospels include several significant events in the life of Jesus that took place there, making it a major site for Christian pilgrimages. The southern part of the mountain, which has been used as a Jewish cemetery for more than three millennia, reportedly contains more than 100,000 graves and remains an important site for modern Jews.

[97] The reader may question Jesus' motives in defying the religious leaders of the people of his day, since he clearly wanted all Jews to believe he was sent by God. However, Jesus knew they would not hear his message.

[98] The Sanhedrin, from the Greek word for "assembly" or "council" was a group of between twenty and twenty-three church members appointed in every city in Judea to decide on all matters of Jewish law. In Jerusalem, the Sanhedrin had seventy-one members and was referred to as the "Great Sanhedrin." Their decisions, including those on capital offenses, were binding, even on the rulers of Israel.

[99] The reader is no doubt aware that the "cornerstone" is traditionally the first stone set and determines the placement for all the remaining stones when a building's foundation is constructed. For this reason, it was the most important stone in the structure. Now its importance is only symbolic and used as part of a dedication of ceremony of a project. Jesus understood the original meaning well, which is why he choose to use the term when he addressed the religious leaders. Luke 20:9-17 uses the word "capstone," which refers to the keystone of an arch, which when set, allows for the construction above it to be supported.

[100] Elijah's raising of a dead child (1 Kgs. 17:17-24) and resurrection accounts in 2 Kgs. 4:16-18, 32-37, and 2 Kgs. 13:21.

[101] Jesus' words here echo those recorded in Ex. 3:6. In addition, Jews, Christians and Muslims believe that Abraham is both the physical and spiritual father of all three faiths and that his son Isaac and grandson Jacob (who is renamed "Israel" by God) were the progenitors of the Jewish nation (Gn. 16). Abraham had a firstborn son, Ishmael, by a servant, both of whom were sent away. Islamic tradition holds that Ishmael was the father of the Arab nations.

[102] In addition to the Ten Commandments, God gave Moses a series of laws, recorded in Leviticus, covering the religious, judicial, and social conduct of the Jewish people. After Moses had read the laws to the people, he asked for their commitment to adhere to them. Upon their assent, he sprinkled sacrificial blood on them to seal their covenant with God. (This act appears to be the genesis of Jesus words and actions at the time of the "Last Supper." – (Matthew 26:26, Page 150)

[103] In Jewish tradition, it was the custom for a bride to keep a lamp, her veil, and her other things beside her bed, awaiting the groom's call. Before the marriage vows were taken and the union consummated, the bride had to first approve of the man to whom she was to be betrothed, which was signaled by her accepting a glass of wine he offered to her. Once accomplished both would sign a marriage commitment, witnessed by two males who were not related to either the bride or the groom. When those arrangements were completed, the consummation of the union awaited the groom's construction of a honeymoon room in his father's house. This is now symbolized by the *Chuppah*, or canopy, that is characteristic of Jewish weddings. The room had to be well constructed and required the father's approval before it was considered ready for the bride. If asked the date of his wedding the groom would have to reply, "only my father knows", which echoed Jesus words to his disciples in Matthew 24:36.

[104] A talent was not a unit of currency but rather the value given to 6,000 denarii, which equates to between sixteen to twenty years of wages for a common laborer or soldier; in today's terms, somewhere between $300,000 to $400,000.

[105] The word "proselyte" originally referred to a Gentile who was considering conversion to Judaism, and was used in this form by early Christians. "Proselytizing" now refers to the practice of attempting to convert anyone to one's own religious beliefs or point of view.

[106] Merton, Robert King. *Science, Technology, and Society in Seventeenth-Century England*, New York: H. Fertig, 1970. Print.

[107] Luke uses the words "*New Covenant*" (Luke 22:20). Throughout the Gospels Jesus is shown quoting scripture. His use here of the term "covenant" is clearly a direct reference to the *Book of the Covenant* (Exodus. 24:7), which contains the religious, legal, moral, and cultural laws of the Jewish faith, as given to Moses by God. After reading it aloud to the people, who swore an oath to obey, Moses splashed sacrificial blood on them saying "This is the blood of the covenant which the LORD has made with you according to all these

words." (Exodus. 24:8)

[108] Roman Catholic, Orthodox, and some other Christian denominations (notably Lutheran) recall Jesus' words during the central part of their religious services and teach that their recitation by an ordained priest consecrates the bread and wine placed upon the altar, allowing those partaking in "communion" (the term derives from the act of the parish communing with Jesus) to receive the actual body and blood of Jesus. Other Christian denominations believe the celebration is symbolic and the communicant receives Jesus in spirit, rather than in substance. The Roman Catholic Church teaches that the transformation is a "mystery of faith," and while the physical appearance to the senses remains unchanged, the *substance* of bread and wine is changed into the body and blood of Jesus. Saint Augustine said that Christians must have faith that the bread and wine are in fact the body and blood of Jesus, despite what they see with their eyes and taste with their mouths. To better contemplate this mystery, some Christians try to envision themselves at the table with the Apostles, receiving bread and wine from Jesus, as they did. For a Christian, there is no more humbling an experience.

[109] See notes 102 and 107 above.

[110] For a description of Sanhedrin see Note 98

[111] While there is historical evidence that Jesus was crucified, some have questioned whether there is evidence that he was scourged, beforehand, which would give credence to the Gospel accounts of his death within hours of his crucifixion. However, given the likelihood of concern for the reaction of his followers, as described hereunder, and the fact that all four Gospels record Pilate's intent to have him flogged, it can be reasonably assumed that Jesus was scourged to hasten his death and burial before the start of the Sabbath.

[112] The cross, in its many forms, is the most recognized symbol of Christianity. While Christian, Anglican, Lutheran and Eastern Orthodox Churches often display the crucified figure of Jesus on the cross to emphasize his sacrifice for humanity, Protestant and other Christian denominations only show the cross, which is symbolic of Jesus' Resurrection. While the Gospels do not describe the cross, virtually all depictions that have come down to us show a cross consisting of a long vertical post and a shorter horizontal crossbeam. However, historians now agree that the condemned would have only carried a horizontal beam, or *Patibulum*, which weighed about one hundred pounds. The *Patibulum* would have a slot carved in it that

would fit on a projecting member of a vertical post, or *Stipes*, which was permanently set in the ground.

[113] The Roman historian Tacitus records that the city of Rome had a specific place for carrying out executions, situated outside the Esquiline Gate, and a specific area reserved for the execution of slaves by crucifixion (Annales 15:60.1, *thelatinlibrary.com* [retrieved 12 December 2009]). We can draw a conclusion from this that a similar location would have been located outside Jerusalem, which the Gospels identified as "Golgotha," or "the place of the skull."

[114] The Romans used forged iron spikes, typically between five and seven inches long, to pin the condemned to the cross, but also used rope to minimize damage to the *Patibulum* where wood was scarce, or to prolong the suffering of the individual, either due to the nature of the crime or to use it as an example to others, such as in the case of a slave. Historical accounts of the Roman's razing of Jerusalem in AD 70 record that many of the condemned were nailed to crosses. The spikes would have been driven through the wrists and feet with the knees bent so that the condemned would be forced to rise up to breathe. While depictions of the crucifixion show the nails driven through the palms of Jesus' hands, it is now known that crucifixions were done with nails driven through the wrists. As entered earlier, since the Aramaic language did not have a separate word for the hand and wrist, the error is understandable.

[115] F. P. Retief and L. Cilliers, *The History and Pathology of Crucifixion, pages 938-41.* South African Medical Journal 93, no. 12 (2003).

[116] As exhaustive asphyxia progressed, the condemned would have found it more and more difficult to breathe or speak. This could explain the brevity of Jesus' last words.

[117] These accounts were copied from lost original documents by a later historian, Sextus Julius Africanus. *Chronographiai* (the *History of the World*), therefore proof of the events is not a historical certainty, as is Jesus' crucifixion.

[118] In 2009 National Geographic published an article which cast doubt on the authenticity of the Shroud, based on the discovery in Israel of the mummified remains of a man who died in the first century, whose body was wrapped in a burial cloth not unlike the shroud. The report's conclusions were based, in part, on the fact that the burial cloth uncovered was of a different fabric and that the weave was much simpler than the Shroud. The report also stated that since it was the only burial cloth discovered to date in the region it was assumed to be the "best" example of the type of burial

cloth that would have been used at the time Jesus died. Finally, on an unrelated matter, the report stated that the sophisticated herringbone 3-on-1 pattern used in the Shroud was not possible until the advent of wooden looms some 1,000 years following Jesus' death. These conclusions were challenged in the 2010 report, which called attention to the fact that the 2009 report stated that it was based on a single discovery, and that the fibers used to make the burial cloth were not native to the region.

Contrasting this, testing done on the Shroud showed it was interwoven with cotton fibers that are only found in the Mideast region, and that no wooden fibers were found, which would have been the case if wooden looms had been used. Moreover, the 2010 report includes a listing of several ancient fabrics discovered in the mid-east region, including one used by the Essenes (See Page 28), which were made using a similarly difficult herringbone type weave employed in the Shroud.

There is an anecdote that comes to mind about the matter – it tells of a nation that proudly proclaimed that it was the first to discover the telegraph, because it had uncovered wires while excavating an ancient "Tell." An adjoining nation responded that a similar excavation in its territory proved it was the first to invent the radio, because no wires were found.

[119] Perhaps it's because he chooses to remain so; and perhaps because he knows that our senses can be easily fooled and "seeing" is not always "believing;" witness those who still refuse to believe Neil Armstrong stepped onto the Moon in 1969. Also, if God wished to prove to us that he existed, wouldn't he need to manifest this to every one of us in some fashion, and do so for each new generation? Perhaps, Jesus was right; perhaps "knowing" something is not as powerful a motivation as "believing," for the former only employs the five senses, which are continually dulled by time and the world, whereas believing in something cannot be willed, it must come from within.

[120] The above words are the genesis of the words most Christians use when making the sign of the cross on their head and breast.

[121] "Fetters" is an old English word for a chain or shackle, used to hobble a person or animal by their feet. While I have come across another version that reads, "And they cling to me, appealing from their fathers," this line makes less sense and may have been corrected at some point from an earlier printing.

[122] The aria is a "duettino" taken from the third act of Mozart's The *Marriage of Figaro (Sull'aria? Che soave zeffiretto)*. As I recalled the

scene I could not help but think of how great works of music and art can capture our senses and release us from ourselves, even if only for a few moments. Incidentally, Mozart was a devout Catholic and wrote many Masses and Liturgical works.

CPSIA information can be obtained
at www.ICGtesting.com
Printed in the USA
BVHW08*0930280818
524792BV00012B/9/P

9 780998 310947